M000189623

ELIZABETH FOTINOPOULOS

YOUR HIDDEN TRUTH

Identifying Life Obstacles and Overcoming Them

ISBN 978-1-54399-660-9 (softcover)
ISBN 978-1-54399-661-6 (ebook)

THOUGHTS, OBSERVATIONS,
&
PRACTICE REGARDING:

Parents
Relationships
Love
Work
Children
Health
Your Potential

A NOTE FROM THE AUTHOR

Readers are advised to proceed with attentiveness. You will be invited to seriously examine your life. A willingness to be honest with yourself and to make necessary changes will be key to your success. Happy reading.

CONTENTS

To my wonderful and loving son Jimmy, who is my guiding light.

To my grandmother,
who always believed in my gift and encouraged me to accept it.

And to all the beautiful spirits
that continue to give me strength and insight.

"*The most beautiful thing we can experience is the Mysterious—the knowledge of the existence of something unfathomable to us, the manifestation of the most profound reason coupled with the most brilliant beauty.*"

—ALBERT EINSTEIN

YOUR HIDDEN TRUTH

We have at least one. What is it? Very simply, it's something you can't see. It could be a talent, a wish, a dream, a fear, a trauma. It could be an event you'd rather forget, or a reality you can't accept. At times, it's an intuition that you simply ignore because it doesn't fit your plans. It can also be something you can't see about someone else. In turn, you act on blind faith. But that blindness inevitably leads to a collision with the unavoidable wall of truth.

Being true to oneself is the most important task in life. It's not a new concept, but remarkably difficult to embrace. Open your heart and mind to what I'm about to share with you. Embrace the possibility that you have a hidden truth, a truth that could be the difference between complacency and a life of total fulfillment.

PART I

ME (ELIZABETH)

MY FIRST VISION

'm five years old, sitting at the foot of the stairs. I hear people coming in and out of our home. They're here visiting my family. As they enter, I feel myself *becoming* them.

"Ely," my mother calls out to me. "Where are you? Let's eat!"

I sit down and she explains. "People are coming to visit. I'll be busy. I want to take care of you and your grandmother."

We sit at the table, say our prayers and enjoy our meal. My grandmother sits with me. She and I spend lots of time together. But now, I say to myself, I need to go to the living room. This is where our family and friends have gathered. They talk and enjoy their time together. I walk between people, feeling as though I've entered them. It's a cold but powerful feeling; the things I see are more important than the wonder and fear of the unknown.

Then, without knowing why, I feel the urge to pick someone. My grandmother, who is also gifted, expects this. She feels my anxiousness. Eventually, I choose a woman. She's happy, completely unaware of the trauma that's about to overpower her. She notices me as I approach. I see fear in her eyes, tears and pain. The closer I get, the clearer her pain becomes. I sit next to her.

"I'm so happy you're here," I say. "I'm very sorry about the death of your husband. But you still have time. Talk to him. Tell him you love him. That will make him happy and it will make you feel better."

"What?" she asks. "Why are you telling me this?"

She looks at my grandmother. She wants to understand, but also doesn't. My grandmother reassures her.

"She needs to tell you this. Please remember what she's said. I hope it helps you. My granddaughter is very special."

"I don't understand," the woman says. She becomes upset. "My husband seems fine—no complaints, no pain, nothing. Thank you, but I must leave."

She stands up and looks at me, utterly confused. As she leaves, my grandmother takes my hand and walks me to our room.

"There are things people prefer not to know," my grandmother says. "I know you feel you must, but it's important to wait until you have been asked. You are special—very special. But you must learn to wait."

A few weeks pass and my prediction comes true: the woman's husband dies. I remember hearing about it and the realization afterward. I did not choose or prepare for this; it's simply how I was born.

MY HIDDEN TRUTH

often ask myself: Are you satisfied? Are you living the way you should? What's your purpose? I struggle with these questions, as I know many people do. Most people who know me don't believe I struggle with anything. But the truth is that we all struggle. I will share my struggle with you.

Perhaps the biggest influence in my life was my grandmother, Elisa. She was powerful, the anchor of our family. She raised us with her great cooking, beautiful singing, and her devout faith. I was named for her. She was my guide throughout life. Among the many lessons she taught me, one of the most important was persevering through misfortune. She became a widow at thirty-nine; her husband—my grandfather—was killed in a trucking accident. In that moment, she became everyone's grandmother. She never remarried. "I'm still married," she liked to say, as though my grandfather stood beside her. She always maintained her optimism despite painful circumstances.

Rather than dwell on her pain, Elisa helped people who needed it. She was compassionate and faithful when others were not. She listened when people chose not to. She understood the complexity of humanity, and helped everyone, no matter the circumstances. As a result, all of us—children, grandchildren, cousins, aunts, uncles—looked to her for counsel. I later discovered that one reason was because she was uncannily successful at reading Tarot cards. A constant stream of neighbors and friends made appointments to hear her readings. But she never accepted payment, refusing it for what she considered a God-given gift. When I was a teenager, I began earning money and every penny went to my grandmother. She immediately gave it to others who were less fortunate. "It will make sense to you later," she told me.

My grandmother taught me the importance of helping others. Her friends described her as the richest poor woman they knew. She also inspired confidence.

"You must believe in yourself," she said. "If you don't, no one will."

It took me a while to appreciate that lesson.

MY TRUE NATURE

From the time I was young I've had the ability to read people and practically everything in their lives. I see milestones and consequences. I see events that *have happened* and events that *might happen.*

I didn't understand it at first. I struggled to grasp how any of it was possible, yet I embraced it. People laughed and shrugged it off as the fantasies of a young child. Then my predictions started coming to fruition. The laughter stopped. Soon people began asking to visit the child who could "see." Some resented it, but I still spoke. I knew intuitively that I could help them. Sometimes the news wasn't good, but it was always something that needed to be said.

I remember people reacting viscously, sometimes with confusion, fear, and even anger. It made me cautious. But my mother and grandmother encouraged me. They knew it wouldn't be easy, but also that it was something that I shouldn't ignore. They considered it a talent; the way Mozart composed music, or the way Einstein conceived theories. Like them, I could see well beyond the typical ability.

Still, it was my hidden truth for many years. As I became older, I lived like a normal person. I went to school, graduated, and joined the workforce. I became the first female Service Manager for General Motors in the United States and Europe. I was quickly promoted to Director of both programs. When that was no longer satisfying, I went to work behind-the-scenes in government and politics. I enjoyed lots of success, and it was exciting. But in my heart, I felt incomplete. Working with people was important to me. There was so much more I could do. I worried about overstepping boundaries and offending my superiors. It kept me silent for many years until, finally, I embraced what I'd been denying for so long.

Accepting my hidden truth—my true nature—set me free and put me on a path of true fulfillment. It wasn't easy. I took a big chance. People tend to look at people who do what I do with lots of suspicion. They judge what they don't understand. In that sense, people often look at me with cautious optimism, excited by the positives and turned off by the negatives. Some go as far as to reject the legitimacy of what I do. I decided long ago that I couldn't worry about negativity. I needed to honor my gift and how I was born. *I needed to honor my true nature.* You too must honor your nature.

MY MISSION

My purpose today is to help people who have lost their purpose. Today, I facilitate positive outcomes for the people I work with. I connect them to their deepest wishes and guide them toward fulfillment.

To achieve fulfillment, people need to feel a sense of purpose. They need to feel as though their gifts work toward the greater good. That's one of the reasons I wanted to share my gift. Over many years, and with hundreds of positive experiences with my clients, I decided that it was time. For years I helped people on an individual basis. I gave advice to friends and family, or gentle warnings to unsuspecting co-workers. From that point on, they'd seek advice. I obliged because it came easily to me. I looked at the source of their problems and advised accordingly. Some would follow my advice and others wouldn't. The success stories were shared with other friends, and those friends would ask for advice. There was no shortage of people who needed guidance. The larger question I struggled to answer: How could I help *everyone*? I needed to reach more people. That's when I began this book. I began looking at fundamental problems that everyone deals with each day and realized that a book could serve as a guide.

I believe that every problem has a solution. Ask yourself: Are you fulfilled? Are you maximizing your potential? Do you make a difference in other people's lives? I work hard to realize my full potential each day, with a goal to make an enormous difference. It's time you do too. You're reading this book because you want answers. You're looking for a better life, and, by extension, a better life for those around you. The first and most important lesson is to take ownership of it. Let's work together to achieve the life you were meant to live, the life you will create by honoring yourself and the people around you. Let's work together to find *your* life. Let's begin our most important journey—the journey of self-discovery and self-actualization. This book is a road map for people who want to discover who they really are, and how to lead the life they want to live.

PART II

YOU (THE READER)

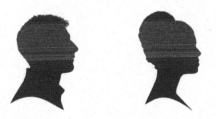

BELIEVE IN YOUR DREAMS, MAKE THEM YOUR REALITY

We all have dreams and we must recognize the power to believe in them. Instead, I often see fear—fear of truth, fear of facts, fear of the unknown. Fear is the predominant force that shapes impossible thinking, which inevitably leads to varying degrees of depression. That leads to lost hope, a loss of motivation, and unsatisfying routines that put outside forces in charge. The negativity feeds off itself and builds like a disease.

The question my clients often ask: What can I do to fix it? This is when I "read" them. It's like watching a movie. I see everything from beginning to end. I watch closely, trying to understand when and why they gave up on happiness. The more I read, the more I see what troubles them. Either they don't know where they're going or feel they don't have the power to overcome their obstacles. People live lives of resignation. They defeat themselves without even trying. They start life with youthful optimism, but something robs them. They don't remember what they want!

In our desperate need to keep up with expectations, we lead ourselves into desperate debt—literal and metaphorical. It becomes a game of basic survival. We tell ourselves that we don't have time for the challenges of life that seem insurmountable. We don't have time for unpleasant surprises or unexpected gambles. Surviving day-to-day is all we can handle; if we are spending our time paying debts, how can we carve out time for self-examination? We give up so easily without even trying.

You have dreams. You've had them since you were young, the types of dreams that inspired your true interests. I can literally see them. And I can see the moment when you gave up and life stopped, the moment your life suspended in air and you convinced yourself that you have changed, the moment you lost your belief and enthusiasm. It stuck in your mind and you don't know it. To overcome it, you need to fundamentally change the way you think.

I walk through crowded spaces, feeling the energy of the people around me. They go about their daily routines. I see so many stories. I see different people, yet so similar. They're going somewhere, doing something, but many have lost faith. They serve a hidden master. It could be a boss, a lover, a husband, a wife, a parent or even a child. They could be serving a lifestyle by living beyond their means. But the most powerful of them all is hundreds of years older and more powerful than anything else. It's *apathy*, the indifference to high ideals or the ability to change the course of your life. It's a willingness to accept defeat rather than fulfill what you believe is right. Apathy has dominated many people for a long time. I see people, young and old, whose decisions have been made for them.

They don't focus on their dreams; the dream is too personal. They think:

My dream is not reality.
My dream might fail.

The problem is that we've convinced ourselves that dreams are too risky. We fear failure, and therefore the effort to try. The other problem is that people dream in perpetuity. It's incumbent upon all of us to make our dreams come true and see them through.

I encourage my clients to define their success by writing it down. It's a simple but amazingly effective practice, and it's a practice that people preach all the time. The reason: It's a manifestation of the thoughts you unwittingly know exist but fail to acknowledge. *Success is the belief in your future. Success is living your life according to your terms, not the expectations of someone else. Success is accepting that life changes at every turn; nothing is fully defined. So many people let life dictate the terms rather than the other way around, and it's a wasted opportunity of the unique qualities that life begs of you. Simply put, there is no one else like you and you need to accept that something uniquely good is in all of us.

Have you stopped listening to your impulses and wishes? Most people don't consider their wishes because they accept their circumstances without question. Throughout history people are taught to cooperate. To many, authority shouldn't be questioned, doubted, or challenged. But what is authority? Who is the author? Do you agree? You must change your concept of authority so that you become the author of your destiny.

You are the master of your destiny rather than a slave to what others decide for you. But you must first learn how you became a slave to the decisions of others.

FEAR, APATHY, AND COOPERATION

wonder why so many people are willing to give up on their life so easily. Perhaps it's because they've been traumatized, and they fear it will happen again—something so bad that it cripples them forever.

I was abandoned as a child.

My parents always criticized me.

I was humiliated in public.

I'm handicapped.

I was rejected.

I was betrayed.

My parents divorced.

I witnessed something horrible.

My lover left me.

I made the worst mistake of my life.

Or maybe it's because of something someone told them.

You must be content with what you're given.

You don't have any talents.

Are you a fool? Why are you taking chances? Be careful!

You must marry so-and-so;
love is unimportant; your future must be secure.
You're not an attractive person. You will struggle in life.

Maybe they were told something more powerful than the belief in their own thoughts and ideas.

When will you grow up?
You're a dreamer! You will never succeed.
Why are you so stupid? You will never understand.

Or perhaps they were given praise before it was warranted.

You will have many successes.
You will be very rich.
You are beautiful. You are blessed.
You are a genius.
You will lead a charmed life.

You may have been told that you are who you are and that you must accept it. Or you may have been told to cooperate or you will pay a price. Whether the prediction is positive or negative is irrelevant; they both stop you from acting. The logic here is that life has been decided for you, and therefore you don't need to do anything. You fear contradicting the people you consider to be wiser than yourself. You conform rather than create the life you want. You cooperate instead of taking the lead. You believe life is easier when you cooperate with other people's wishes. It's the very idea that your future has already been determined without your participation that robs you of the life you want. Imagine an idea robbing you of life, or the ability to choose, the desire to succeed, the wish to be happy. It seems absurd, wouldn't you say? We must change this way of thinking.

People accept these predictions as unchangeable. The question is: Why? You essentially agree that you have no voice in shaping your future. You see no reason to dream about the life you want. You've given up. This is an unacceptable choice! There are consequences for all our actions, and there is no sense choosing a defeating path when there are so many other possibilities to choose from.

I can see both the negative and positive outcome of a decision you might make. I never understand why people choose the negative path. But what I've learned and what I continue to see is that most people believe they don't have a choice. It pains me. I see many people slowly and unwittingly destroying themselves simply by thinking this way. It can't continue. The world can't be filled with hopelessness. We must have the courage to change our thinking to effect positive change in the world, or negativity will destroy us.

REMOVING BAD HABITS

You say that it's not within your power. You say that your situation is different and that it can't be changed. You say that something has been a certain way for years, and therefore can't change. You believe that you had a difficult childhood, or that someone you love doesn't love you in return. You believe that you've tried and failed too many times, or that you don't have the money to achieve what you want. You say you don't have the time, or that you have too many responsibilities. You believe it's impossible to help yourself. You believe that nothing will ever change. To you, there's always a reason that you can't, *because* ...

There are countless excuses for not taking control of your life. Stop making excuses. Take responsibility for your circumstances. Begin life anew. Remove the negativity that's become the theme song of your life.

NEGATIVITY, ADDICTION, AND PESSIMISM

N egative thinking is a habit. If you start your day complaining, you'll probably end it that way. It becomes a part of your personality. Some people might find this trait amusing or comforting (misery loves company), but it's the kind of trait that prevents you from making necessary changes. Negativity is learned, a response to rejection. It's a protective mechanism that eventually becomes self-destructive.

If I don't hope for success, then I can't be disappointed.
I'll never meet the right person. They're all the same.
Why bother looking?

Negativity is also an addiction. It takes over your body and its power grows. And as it grows, your dependence on it grows. You feel like you need more to satisfy a craving. You practice negative thinking so much that it becomes second nature, and you don't realize that you're suddenly at its mercy. Negative thinking also attracts other negative thinkers. They increase in numbers and strength. They ridicule optimists. Negative thinkers even pride themselves on their negativity and cynicism, worshiping at the altar of pessimism.

You don't have control over your destiny.
Your wishes are meaningless.
There is no justice.
You're arrogant and a fool if you think you can change anything.
You must accept what you've been given.
You can't change anything.

Sound familiar? It's mostly arrogance telling you what is and what isn't possible. Those people attract what they put into the world, a sense of hopeless negativity. Submitting to their will once again lets apathy become your master.

I'm here to tell you that they're wrong. You can change as much as you wish to change. But you must take charge. When was the last time you had a negative thought? I challenge you to do everything in your power to avoid a negative thought for twenty-four hours. Observe how negativity creeps in your mind or attitude throughout the day. Write it down. Compare it to the frequency of positive thoughts. Now, turn it around! Choose the way you think. Develop optimistic habits and positive thinking. It will be difficult at first because it's hard to shake addictions. Do it one step at a time until you've shifted the balance of your thinking to positive thoughts. Remember that you're not alone; many people suffer from negative thinking. When you begin doubting the power of positivity, think of the people who've overcome great odds and negativity to achieve the seemingly impossible.

"We stand here today as nothing more than a representative of the millions of our people who dared to rise up against a social system whose very essence is war, violence, racism, oppression, repression and the impoverishment of an entire people."

—NELSON MANDELA

"Inevitably, an individual is measured by his or her largest concerns."

—NORMAN COUSINS

"You gain strength, courage and confidence by every experience in which you really stop to look fear in the face. You are able to say to yourself, 'I have lived through this horror. I can take the next thing that comes along.' You must do the thing you think you cannot do."

—ELEANOR ROOSEVELT

"You must be the change you want to see in the world."

—GANDHI

"All that we are is what we have thought."

—BUDDHA

Can you name the positive thinkers in your life? Are your role models optimists? Are they achievers? Which are you?

UNDERSTAND THE FORCES THAT SHAPED YOU

t's within your power to create the life you want rather than accepting life as it has been shaped for you. This will require work on your part; you've spent many years teaching yourself how to behave. It will require time and effort to examine and correct mistakes. To shape your future, you must have the courage to face the past. You need to see clearly to act. I say "clearly" because our vision is often clouded when our memories are painful. But how you see the past is critical to the kind of decisions you make. Your decisions form your future. Let's dismantle the obstacles created by others. Some might say that your future will be difficult. Yes! That's probably what *they* see. But how many tell you that change is possible? I've helped many people avoid unhappy futures. I've helped people identify their obstacles and given voice to their hidden desires and dreams. Miraculous transformations take place for people willing to take ownership of their life and carve a new path. How do you get on that path? First, you must know who you are.

You are the culminating result of many forces. From the time you're born, and even before then, there are seen and unseen hands shaping the beginning of your life—your parents, their parents, teachers, friends, and neighbors. By the time you become an adult, you forget those forces are there. Your tendency is to blame yourself for everything that's negative or positive, even though all of it depends on *how* you came into this world. You start life with infinite possibilities and the world begins shaping those possibilities. Your wishes are never understood or properly considered until after the dye's been cast. You hope that your guardians did their best, but that's not always the result. You must never forget that yearning and desiring success comes at the very moment of birth; it's an intrinsic part of your holistic self. What people forget is that it's always a part of you, and if it becomes lost, it can be found again.

Let me give you an example. A client of mine, Daniel, had his life mapped out by his loving parents. He would be groomed to become a businessman and he would eventually inherit the family business. Unfortunately, Daniel's parents overlooked his true passion and dream—aeronautics. Daniel was obedient, respectful, and grateful. He honored his parents rather than accept his nature. Still, he loved anything that could fly. At a certain point, he felt lost. He asked for my help. We spent many hours talking about his family, his childhood, and his true passion. It took time, but he eventually accepted his passion. Aeronautics was a vital part of his being, but he reluctantly showed it and was worried about his parents. He confided to me that they'd be upset, and he was correct. To them, it was a complete disruption of their well-structured plan. I met with Daniel's parents, and, with my guidance, they accepted Daniel's plan to follow his dream. They wanted the best for him, no matter what they'd planned. Today, Daniel is an aeronautics engineer—a very successful one. He discovered his hidden truth and now honors his true nature. He's happy. Daniel's parents are also very proud.

ASSESSMENT AND JUDGMENT

A human being forms inside a woman. It's life at its most beautiful and unadulterated stage. However, how the child turns out is full of risk. *You* are at risk even before birth. The physical and emotional circumstances of the mother can have a profound effect on the unborn child. Then there's the added confusion of what people expect from this creation. Some may consider a new human being to be perfect while others may not. The way a child develops depends very much on how the individual's parents think of themselves. Parents are affected by their parents, their grandparents by their parents, etc. It's an unending chain of positive and negative forces affecting our lives. This is the power of ancestry. From the point of conception, everything is dictated to this new "creation of infinite possibility." You're told how to behave, what to do, how to survive. Sometimes the information is good and sometimes it's not. The child cannot discern which is which. You have no control. You don't develop the skills necessary to keep your hope-filled life on track. From the moment you're born, your parents try to teach you how to function independently. But that isn't necessarily what happens. Parents have their own fears, and they can get in the way of that transition.

You are my precious child.
You must believe everything I say.
Your survival depends on listening to me.

It's not just parents that are responsible for perpetuating a paradoxical fear. Teachers and guardians do it too. They force children into a state of arrested development, creating a false perception that their approval is the only thing that matters in life. While you're growing up—especially the early years—you're put through countless tests; you are assessed:

You are intelligent/not intelligent.
You are pretty/not pretty.
You will be successful/unsuccessful.

These are early predictions and sometimes they're the most damaging. You hear them and start living them through the power of suggestion, as children try to emulate what their parents teach them, directly or indirectly, both positive and negative lessons.

As an example, children learn honor from their parents. If they're taught to behave honorably (like being honest or honoring one's word), they'll appreciate honor when it's absent from their lives. Then how do children learn to lie? The answer is the same. Parents may think that their deceits are hidden, but they underestimate the intelligence and awareness of children, who may see their parents interact beautifully with the world but also see them behave differently behind closed doors. Suddenly the adult isn't so perfect; they have no time for the child, no time for their spouse; what they portray to the world is different from reality. Their behavior is a lie. A child learns to behave in the same manner, and soon they've learned how to be dishonest. It's odd to think that children are too young to notice certain behaviors, but they do. It's part of a child's education.

After you've gone through formal schooling, it's time to show off your achievements and how you plan to make your way in the world. You are judged. That's when *you*, the former child, start to quantify your worth.

I am a success.
I am a failure.

But you forgot about the beginning. You forgot about your teachers. What we fail to recognize is that the process of becoming an adult is the culmination of many people, many circumstances, and many fates. Instead of thinking *I*, people should be thinking *we*.

We succeeded.
We failed.

IDENTIFYING SIGNIFICANT PEOPLE
AND MOMENTS IN YOUR LIFE

D o you remember when life stood still? Before judging yourself, you must know who you are and the elements that made you. You must identify the pivotal moments and key players in your life. As you train for independence an event (or several) occurs that stops the awareness of your wishes. Think of the damaged child that lives at the mercy of another. Think of the domineering parent, or the parent that behaves more like a child.

There are many variations that stop a child's growth. Let's go to the next step in our investigation of what happened to you. Let's go back to the moment *you* decided that you were a success or a failure. If you believe you were a failure, I want you to feel that pain again. I want you to relive that moment. I want you to understand what happened. I want you to view it from a distance. I want you to identify *why* you felt that way. You might think to yourself:

It was my fault!
I'm ugly.
I'm bad.

Why do you feel this way? Was anyone else involved? Why do you believe you're unworthy of a success? Think about it in detail and ask yourself why you're being self-defeating. Beauty is subjective. Beauty is also a standard that people set for themselves. Your perception of beauty is what stands in your way. It can't be measured in any specific way. As for thinking that you're bad, this is one of the most damaging of self-criticisms. It's an acknowledgement that you deserve to be punished. Let's revisit all those moments and feelings, but *not with the intention of blaming someone or something.* Above all, don't make harsh judgments. Leave the past there so it doesn't interfere with your future.

Let's go back to that point when life stood still. Let's redo anything that feels unsatisfying, whether it be a relationship, parents, opportunities, a wrong direction, or the people around us. We want to go back to that moment and start from the point when destiny can no longer dictate our doomed future. Once we know our mistakes and what we perceive to be failures, we can transform and correct things by not repeating them. Now go back to that feeling again and remember who was involved, who was present, and who was responsible. What were the forces that helped make it happen that way?

IDENTIFYING THE EARLY SUCCESSES

Remember when life was good? To correct our mistakes, we must also know our successes. We've all had some form of success. Relive it, no matter how trivial it may seem. You must remember the powerful *feeling of success*. Think about the good grades you received at school. Think about the time you designed something beautiful that made your parents proud. Think about the race you won in high school. Think about the problem you solved that no one else could. Think about the smile you brought to someone's face for a good deed.

Positivity is a powerful feeling. We should repeat that feeling. Each day you make a positive change, each day you take charge of your life is a day filled with success. This is a feeling we need to experience again and again. You must also remember that early success can confuse your thinking; you must not feel satisfied with one success alone. Your journey doesn't end with one success. You don't conclude a journey with one small act of kindness. You create your future by making decisions each day, and those decisions happen all the time. You must remain nimble in your thinking, your attitude, and your approach to life's unpredictable nature.

HONORING YOUR TRUE NATURE
AND CHOOSING YOUR MISSION

People shouldn't misunderstand my intentions. Failure can't be attributed to the actions of one's parents alone; there are many people who might be responsible for the way you perceive life as it is. It could be close relatives, or a guardian, or role model. Whatever it is or whoever it might be, the person you choose to become has a lot to do with your upbringing. It has to do with the man or woman that sits on the opposite side of the table you share together. When you come home with something—an idea, a wish, something that makes you happy—but it doesn't mean anything to those at home (the people who brought you into this world, the people who are supposed to encourage and love you), you begin to think that your love and passion means nothing to the rest of the world. That's not a reason to give up on your dream, on yourself, or the decision-making power of your life. If you were never taught to be independent, then *you must teach yourself to be independent.* Your parents did the best they could with what they inherited. Don't judge them. It's important to acknowledge how you were raised, but once you have that information, *you must take responsibility for where you're going.*

Fault and blame are crutches, yet another way of coming up with excuses for not acting. It's easy to blame others for your circumstances, and you're not alone. It's a trap that most people fall into. But we must stop it.

When I work with people, they don't want me to see them as I see them. They want me to see their problems. They want me to connect their problems to other people they feel are responsible for those problems. They don't want me to judge them, and they don't want to believe that they share some responsibility for those problems. They want to look good in my eyes. But what I do is look at people the way they refuse to look at themselves. I look at people and see the flaws that we all live with. It's part of being human.

It can be hard for people to hear me speak sometimes. They don't expect me to tell them that they must be responsible for their life. But it's *their* life. They can't—and shouldn't—expect anyone else to live their life for them. Of course, that's assuming they're living and not simply existing. There's a big difference between living and existing. Those who don't understand what I mean by "living" just continue existing. They call it living even though it has nothing to do with what they want, what they desire or what they care about. So, they look for someone to blame for their unhappiness. Many people do this. They believe there's an unspoken reason for the problems in their life, and in turn, they give other people complete power over their future.

My life is a mess because of him/her.

On some level, it's almost ridiculous to think this way. Somewhere along the line you've fallen off track and given your life away, which will eventually make you bitter and angry. Once you do something that you don't want to do, you become unhappy. *And if you're unhappy, you can't make anyone else happy.*

This is probably the most exciting and most difficult part of your journey toward self-discovery. You're born with a gift. We're all born with a gift. That gift is an intrinsic part of your nature, your unadulterated nature. But sometimes your gift, your talent, can be overlooked or neglected. Or, in my case, put on hold. Sometimes it's suppressed by those who don't see its value, or, simply, by those that envy you. Regardless, you must understand that you have it. You must believe that everyone has a unique gift. Part of the journey of life is discovering, recognizing, and nurturing that talent. It doesn't have to be something spectacular or uncanny. It can be something very subtle. Think of the person who is fascinated by things that can't be seen by the naked eye, who might one day discover something vitally important for the survival of humanity. Think of the nurse at the hospital who humbly holds your hand with exquisite care and sensitivity while your doctor attempts to cure you. Both people are vitally important for your wellbeing. All people have gifts, and they must nurture them.

Identifying this gift, your true nature, is not as easy as it sounds. You must pay attention to yourself. It's important that you accomplish this to be fulfilled as an individual. There's a process in discovering, or uncovering, your true nature—your hidden truth. It goes together with deciding your purpose in life.

I have seen so many people who have gone in a direction that wasn't in their nature. Even financial success does not make them truly happy. Conversely, I have seen extraordinary happiness in people who reconnect with who they really are.

Of course, you must remember that true happiness comes from sharing your gift with others. It provides a sense of purpose, the giving of your gift. It can be something as simple as choosing to serve your community. You might ask yourself how your love of animals can serve your community, or how your love of numbers can serve mankind. You might believe your dreams don't follow the status quo, and how they might serve humanity. This is for you to discover. This will be the definition of your success. Once you identify your purpose, you will start to succeed with your relationships as well. Your love and acceptance of your true nature will attract others of like-mind and you'll find your kindred spirit. Many people make the error of looking for an intimate relationship to reflect their true nature. That's like a blind person searching for someone who can see. But how do you know the person you chose can see if you are blind? Because the person says they can see what's best for you? Are they in charge of your life? Have you given them that power over you? And what about their hidden truth? Are you willing to accept who they really are?

If you haven't found independence from your parents, teachers, and friends, if you've not discovered your own mission, then you'll carry that dependence over to your relationship. You'll always seek someone to guide you. You'll be looking for someone to fill the void where your true nature and mission should be in full bloom.

RELATIONSHIPS

The problems that you don't resolve with your parents often carry over into your relationships. This is a hidden burden that you place on an unsuspecting mate. If you grow up feeling that you didn't get enough attention from your mother or father, you'll expect it from your partner. A typical complaint is, "You're not hearing what I'm saying!" But do you realize that you picked a mate with the same characteristics as the parent that didn't listen?

If you didn't get your parents' approval, you'll expect it from your mate. "I'm not needy," you declare. "Mates are supposed to support each other." You're looking for unconditional love and approval. You're trying to solve the original problem you experienced with your parents. People become so involved with relationships:

I can fail at many things, but I won't fail at this.

Instead of looking inwardly at themselves they look to others to solve their feelings of inadequacy. But again, you must look to the source of the pain. Many are trying to shut off the negative voice that can never be satisfied. It might be a parent, a teacher, a friend. Whoever it is, the negativity is all you remember. Many good things may have been said, but it's our nature to remember the negative things. The relationship problems you couldn't solve as a child are carried over to the relationships you establish outside of the home. You're constantly trying to prove your worthiness. You're trying to please or be pleased.

People are yearning to find something they're good at, something that comes so easily that it doesn't feel like work, something that feels natural and good. They want life to be easy, so they pursue a relationship. Seems easy enough. It's natural. The fact is, nature is one of the predominant factors at work. People get comfortable with each other and soon they start a family. Biology is running their lives. But in the back of their mind, they are still yearning to silence the negative voice that says they can't achieve. They believe they can succeed at having a family, which suggests a positive direction, a choice, a commitment, and a sense of responsibility. It's a natural impulse. However, people face a much larger problem if they don't know who they really are.

Take time to renew your commitment to yourself. No matter what stage of the life-journey, it's never too late to start again and live the life you want. Know yourself. We set aside so many things that we intend to do. We call them our goals. This attitude can be detrimental because it implies that goals are difficult or even impossible to achieve.

Let's start again, this time with goals that we can achieve. A long journey starts with the first step. Before you love others, you must learn to love yourself. Before you can please others, you must learn to please yourself. You shouldn't perceive these ideas as being selfish. You're simply being fair. You can't have feelings for others that you've never experienced yourself.

You can pretend that you're happy, which is what so many unhappy people do, but that's not fair to those around you, or even to you. Use yourself as an example so that you're able to help others.

Ask yourself: What do I really want? I don't mean typical things that all people want like love, security, or happiness. I'm referring to the dream you had before you began tackling the things that nature demands. Remember the dream you dismissed as impossible or ridiculous? Did you forget what you really want? Don't let go of that dream. Don't make the same mistake again. Don't do what others want you to do. Take ownership of your life through your actions. Let's move ahead. This is a new time, a new way of thinking. This is a new life. Now is the time to take responsibility, take charge, and make your life what you want it to be. I want that feeling for you, the feeling of authorship. I love that feeling. And then I want you to think about fear and apathy. Do they have a role in your life?

If life has given you a second chance you must take it. The first chance was taken from you. I will not hold you accountable for the things that have happened since then. But now that you have a second chance, there's no one to blame but yourself.

It doesn't matter how old you are. You could be twenty or heading toward your mid-eighties. The day you begin to live life to the fullest, the way you want it to be, is the day you begin living. It could be the last six days, six months, or last hour of your life; you must learn to live life *your* way. *Break the habits that stop your life.*

PRACTICING OPTIMISM

You must make a conscious effort to change the way you think. You must deal with your apathy and fear—your enemies. They stop you. You must battle them. You must *choose a daring, optimistic path and act*. Fear of failure prevents you from choosing your own course. Apathy prevents you from taking any course. Begin each day with specific, achievable goals. Do that six days a week. You'll get a great deal accomplished. Be clear about what you want each day.

- ACHIEVE: Be an achiever as well as a dreamer. By the end of each day, be sure to achieve at least three things that get you closer to realizing your dream.

- SHARE: Enjoy small successes throughout the day. Make your small successes known to those you respect and admire.

- WISH: Envision your reward. It's fair for it to be commensurate with the work you've done.

- **EMPOWER YOURSELF:** Surround yourself with people who stimulate your positive energy. That may include helping people who are stuck in negative energy. If it doesn't take over your life, you can find joy in their positivity.

- **BE PRACTICAL:** Practice measured patience; be willing to change course if you're not moving forward.

- **BE RELIABLE:** Honor your word.

- **BE HELPFUL:** Spend time helping others, which allows you to evaluate yourself in a truthful way.

- **BE RESPECTFUL:** Respect time—your time and the time of others. The less time you think you have, the more you'll appreciate and value the present moment in which you are living.

- **MAINTAIN BALANCE:** Be productive and remember to replenish mind, body, and soul.

- **BE GENEROUS:** Share what you have so you can accept the abundance that surrounds you.

- **BE GRATEFUL:** Give gifts regularly (a sincere smile, perhaps) and learn to accept them.

- **BE INDEPENDENT:** Steer clear of addictions, any and all.

- **BE SUPPORTIVE:** Be a cheerleader for the people close to you.

- **BE A CATALYST:** Do your best to take at least one negative situation each day and turn it around.

- **BE HUMBLE:** Respect everyone's right to an opinion, even if you disagree with it.

- **BE COURAGEOUS:** Don't be seduced by negativity. Trust the path of positive thinking.

Imagine having a parent who guides you in the wrong direction or stops you from going in *any* direction. Or worse still, does everything for you so you never learn how to do things for yourself. Will that serve you in life? In my experience, many people believe they're not capable of achieving their dreams. It's stated—implicitly or explicitly—by their guides. It's an opinion that's embedded in your mind by people who have control over you. You must recognize this problem and turn it around.

But you must act. Apathy is the easy way out. Turning your life over to apathy relinquishes responsibility. Fear prevents you from taking risks and robs you of potential rewards. Take command of your life. Stop blaming your circumstances on others and you'll be on the path to fulfillment and happiness. Be the achiever you were meant to be.

Every problem has a solution. However, you must recognize that you have a problem and that it needs fixing. That's a positive spin on something that needs attention. And it will take time to solve. Have you ever tried to break a habit? It takes time and patience. When you begin to feel overwhelmed, you must understand that you're in charge of your feelings. If you feel comfort by falling into a depression by the challenges before you, then you and your situation will remain static. Depression is something you must fight. If you fight for your happiness, it will come. It's a daily task. Begin the work so that you can live a happy life!

APPRECIATION AND GRATITUDE

Take time to do an inventory of the positive things in your life. Here are just a few examples of the many blessings that make me, and others feel grateful:

I have a purpose and a talent.
I have opportunities to help people.
I have beautiful, loving children.
I have a roof over my head.
I have food on my table.
I have good friends.
I have faith in the power of good.
I have a loyal, caring husband.

Maintaining a positive attitude helps keep people in the worst circumstances alive. There are countless examples of those who withstood pain, torture, imprisonment, even terminal illness, simply because they maintained a positive outlook. No matter how difficult life can be, there's always something for which you can be grateful. There are so many things that you take for granted every day. Recognize your good fortune—be grateful.

And don't pity yourself if you believe you're less fortunate. There are those without eyesight, who have a remarkably keener sense of what's around them. Some people are paralyzed, but they move with their imagination. They adapt. One must fight for a positive outlook. Don't wallow in bitterness by the challenges of poor health. Those who lose their health can appreciate what it means to be healthy; they develop a greater appreciation of life because they know first-hand the fragility of existence. Life is filled with challenges we must overcome. Focus on the positive aspects of any challenge and you'll conquer the debilitating disease of negativity. Be grateful for your parents. Try to understand them. They are human and imperfect—just like all of us! There are many who are unaware of the sacrifices their parents make for them. Some don't realize these things until they become parents themselves. Some never choose to recognize their love, generosity, and sacrifices. Some people feel entitled to these acts of love. Why? Why are they entitled? What makes them exempt from expressing love and gratitude in return? How did they earn the right to punish those who have sacrificed for them? Why do they punish by withholding love when they've been given love? There's a price for this behavior. They don't realize the cost until they feel emptiness in their heart, the place where love should have been maturing over time. Those people feel pain when their parents are gone and it's too late to show gratitude. That will be a greater punishment—the punishment of eternal regret. Learn to recognize people's efforts on your behalf (whether you think they're right or wrong) and be grateful for their good intentions.

After you've taken your inventory of appreciation, you must take time to express your gratitude. Allow this gratitude to bring a smile to your face; carry it with you throughout your journey. The positive energy you emanate will change you and the world around you.

Every day of your life is an achievement. As you wake up, you must be grateful for this life. You must be grateful for standing on your own feet. Be grateful for your dreams and for the things you see and want. There are some who can't dream because they can't see the things that you're now beginning to see. The very fact that you're reading this book to take command of your life is cause for celebration.

PART III

US (CASE STUDIES)

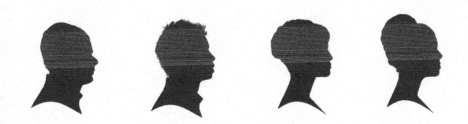

Included here are true stories of people that I've helped. The personal relationships within the stories are complex because each person has a unique journey, their hidden truth. You might recognize your own struggle as you read about their journey.

Love and desire are like water and air—they are necessary.
They can support life or overwhelm you. You must be conscious of what
the elements in your life are doing for you. You must be ready to let
them go if they're not helping you flourish.

BECKY AND GEORGE

The first thing I noticed about Becky and George was their differences.

It's not uncommon for opposites to attract, but it's important that they complement one another. I could see that what connected them in the past couldn't be changed, and events in their future could hurt them and their family.

Becky was in her early forties, George in his mid-thirties. Both were charming and charismatic, equally talented in their artistic pursuits. They were passionate and determined people, always looking beyond the scope of their horizon. It was also clear that their relationship was riddled with challenges. The age difference was significant, and they struggled to overcome it. They were together for almost twelve years when I met them. They had two sons, ages nine and five, whom they adored. Their kids were a powerful unifying bond, a force that allowed them to persevere through difficult times. But ultimately, Becky and George possessed different traits that were obstacles to their happiness. I began by celebrating the joy in their lives.

"Those children are very fortunate to have such caring parents. As I look at them, I feel the love and laughter in your home. There's freedom to explore. There's encouragement. And because of that your sons are confident and secure. They're certainly more fortunate than some. Isn't that right, George?"

"They certainly are," he responded.

"There's nothing you wouldn't sacrifice. Isn't that right, Becky?"

She smiled. "I want to give them everything I can."

"You want them to have every opportunity in life. That's great. You want to help them discover their talents, their strengths."

"Absolutely."

"You want them to succeed in their chosen field, their dream job, yes?"

"Of course."

"And they will. But don't you think the two of you deserve that too?"

They were confused. In their minds, they were following the path they'd chosen.

"We're doing pretty well," George said. "Do you see something different?"

"We'll get back to that."

I paused to give them a moment to think.

"You want what's best for your children, but you don't always agree on what's best. We need to look at what's best for everyone."

I took a piece of paper and a pen and began drawing. As I spoke, I illustrated what I was reading in them. I drew a giant "Y" that filled the page. On one side, I drew several rectangles and on the other side many tiny "X"s.

"I see many projects for both of you. Many. Lots of people are involved. Very different kinds of people. Lots of travel. You'll have to coordinate carefully so that you can both accomplish your tasks and the children are still taken care of as you wish them to be. This will be possible because your projects don't involve the same people. I see many people seeking advice from Becky. George has a desk with many books. He's also writing."

They were pleased and excited. It was important that they focus on the positive aspects of the future because the challenges ahead were not going to be easy.

"You're going in different directions. You should honor that. You both have different needs, different ambitions. You're both independent by nature. Why not follow that impulse? Why waste time arguing? You should follow your own path."

I paused.

"And not only with work. To some degree, you do that with your children. You differ in your philosophy of how to raise them. But there's no need to debate in front of them. It only confuses them."

I paused again to assess their response. I knew this was difficult.

"You're competing with each other, and that will never make you or anyone in the family happy."

They were completely unaware of this.

"You both cling tightly to your point-of-view, even at the cost of hurting each other's feelings."

They looked at each other, acknowledging the truth. They looked back at me.

"Can we fix it?" Becky asked.

"That's up to you."

Twelve years of the same behavior would be difficult to change. The problem started at the beginning of their relationship. When they met, Becky and George were performing with one of the most prestigious dance companies in the world. They worked, traveled, and experienced life together. It was a comfortable partnership for the most part, but they competed. Naturally, this led to resentment.

Competition in a relationship guarantees argument and resentment.

Working and living together exacerbated the situation; allowing some privacy to get relief from the day-to-day tension was nearly impossible. They compromised to maintain peace. But at what cost?

"A loving relationship is not supposed to hurt," I said, finally.

They understood. But only Becky truly understood. It's what she feared. She didn't want to believe it.

"We should look at our priorities," I added. "We must put them in the proper order. It will benefit everyone, especially the children. You must be honest with yourself. Are you living the life you want to live? Are you communicating it clearly?

Once you have answered those questions, you have a chance to be honest with each other."

I couldn't continue because they needed to hear things as individuals rather than as a couple. They needed a better understanding of their personal history. I couldn't give them more ammunition to argue. George suggested we meet again separately, and we all agreed. I left them with an important thought:

"Change is good. Don't fear it. Be afraid of stagnation and unhappiness. Those conditions do greater damage."

I met with George. He was a fierce optimist. He also had a difficult childhood. I read this during our first meeting. Still, he was in better shape than expected. I admired his resiliency. He came far despite a challenging background. Since childhood, he put the needs of others before his own. He needed to understand why. First, I had to introduce him to himself. There were many early dreams that he forgot about. I encouraged him to take the path I saw in his dreams.

"What about the ideas and projects I see buried deep in the last drawer of your desk?" He smiled. He had many ideas that he didn't share with others.

"Really?" he asked. "I never seem to have time to follow through."

"You must make time. But it's not just a matter of time."

"I lose confidence. I don't know why."

"Don't worry," I said. "You will gain confidence as you share your ideas. It's not unlike what you do now."

He smiled.

"Of course," I continued, "it's easier to share when you've been encouraged to do so. A child needs to be heard."

He thought I was referring to his parenting skills when in fact I was referring to his childhood.

"You put so much heart and soul in those writings. Why are you hiding them?"

I could feel his energy rise. His eyes gleamed with excitement. More than anything, he needed encouragement to pursue *his dreams*. It was a wonderful moment. But the core problem—his childhood—had to be addressed with caution. Growing up, he lacked the conditions that every child deserves. He needed unconditional love. His past affected his decision making, and now he was dealing with the consequences of those handicapped choices.

"You've been living your life serving others and ignoring yourself. You've placed all your attention on creating a happy family," I said. "It's a very good goal, but what's motivating it? You're trying to make up for the unhappiness of your childhood."

"My father has a hot temper," he replied. "It drives my family crazy. He and I don't get along. Never have. He explodes about trivial things. It didn't make for a very happy household."

He laughed. It was more relief than amusement. Still, I could feel his sadness. How can a child share his dreams with someone who's impatient? How can a child develop a sense of self-worth if everything is dominated by the needs of another? How can a child share a dream if the people most important to him—his parents—don't have the patience to listen?

with what you understand today. Think of this as an opportunity to move forward in a positive direction."

"And my relationship with Becky? Is she suffering my past?"

"She loves you. She loves that you're a good father to her children. But she doesn't love your restless nature. She doesn't understand it."

"I definitely got that feeling from her."

"You're competing with each other. Competing means someone must win. That's not how a marriage should work. Becky can't help herself. She's been competing all her life. She loves you. Make no mistake. But she's too focused on your journey, your choices. It's not healthy for her or your relationship."

This was hard for George to hear, but he knew it was true.

"Why does she always seem unhappy with my choices and desires? Why is she against my decision to transition to a new field?"

"Hasn't she been following you in that transition? Isn't she trying to do what you're doing?"

He thought for a moment.

"Has it helped?"

"No, because what's right for you isn't necessarily right for her. Becky is competing in an area she can't win. Her performing days are coming to an end. Watching your career confuses her because you're able to take risks. She shouldn't measure your achievements against hers. There are better things ahead for her in other areas."

George sat deep in thought.

"Becky is very different from you. She needs to understand this. You can't expect her to agree if she disagrees. She resists your decisions because she's afraid she won't be able to compete and gain your respect. Again, she has her journey and you have yours. It's time for you to concentrate on your journey and it's time for her to concentrate on hers. Accept your true nature and you will both be happier."

George paused and began confronting what he'd been afraid to face for a long time.

"Can I take some time to process this information?"

"Of course. But remember that too much time has already been spent on this path."

I knew his real concern—the future of the children.

"It will be better for both of you to go on with your lives as individuals rather than as partners. It will ultimately be better for the children as well. You both have a lot to accomplish, but your relationship is standing in the way."

He was torn. He loved his children so much.

"This will cause a lot of disturbance. I don't want to hurt anyone."

"Don't you think you're hurting them more by being dishonest about your relationship? The bond with your children will remain forever. Your family and friends will survive the disappointment; they won't be any happier if you remain unhappy."

"You've given me a lot to think about. I must admit it feels right. We tried to separate several times, but always got back together. To be honest, it hasn't worked very well. There seems to be something so wrong about loving someone and yet not being able to live with them."

"You'll never stop loving each other. But you'll love each other better when you stop arguing and pulling in opposite directions. You should focus on fulfilling your dreams and achieving the success that you're both capable of achieving. Remember: your children are watching; *their future will be formed by the choices you make in life.*"

George promised to call me after he had time to think about our conversation. He also wanted to discuss it with Becky. I didn't mention that she was prepared for that conversation; she just could not say what was on her mind.

Becky was very intelligent. She succeeded as an artist in a field that's highly competitive for a woman—ballet. Even though she was a celebrity in her field, I could see that she wasn't satisfied with her accomplishments. She had a very exciting future ahead, but she was preoccupied with other thoughts. One of the most damaging was the fear that her career had come to an end. She needed to see other possibilities.

"You're a very strong woman. And such a wonderful mother! Those boys are so lucky to have a mother like you. And they love you so much."

She smiled.

"They're my life."

"And that's wonderful. They always will be. They'll do very well because of all you do for them. They'll learn many important lessons from you. They'll remember your strength and courage. You will teach them by example. They will be fine. But what about your dreams? You and I know that there's more for you."

She seemed surprised, as though she'd given up hope for those dreams.

"You mean performing?"

"No. You've realized that part of your dream. You did very well. I'm talking about other dreams."

"I'm not sure I know. I've been a performer for so long ..."

"I mean the part of you that loves nurturing. And not just your children."

Becky thought for a moment.

"I love teaching."

"And you're a wonderful teacher. But there's even more in you. I see you guiding many people, not just students. Not just in a classroom."

Becky laughed.

"I've taught all over the country, if that's what you mean."

"I'm not speaking of your past. It's your future! You're capable of far more than what you've already accomplished, which I know is already extraordinary."

She laughed.

"Actually, I feel like I haven't accomplished anything."

"That's something we'll talk about. But first, I need you to think with a fresh mind. I see people coming to you for answers. You're in charge. But you must believe that you deserve to be in charge."

"I still teach part-time but taking care of the kids is really exhausting. I don't know that I can handle much more."

"You *will* handle much more. You'll see. Eventually, your boys will need you less. It's almost time for them to be with their father. And you'll be ready for what's coming. Great opportunities are coming from unexpected sources. But you must be ready to accept them."

"But my children! I worry about them. I want what's best for them."

"And rightly so. But eventually they must be on their own. Believe me, you will teach them the best lesson by realizing your full potential."

"I worry that George ..."

"You don't need to worry about George. You should be more concerned with yourself. You have so much to offer. You're a very independent woman. Think independently."

She wanted to be independent but was afraid she couldn't. Her self-doubt was damaging amazing potential.

"I've invested so much in the relationship."

"And you are blessed with two beautiful children, whom you both love very much."

"I don't remember how to be independent."

"You've done many things independently. You need to refresh your memory. Didn't you move by yourself to New York City?"

"Yes."

"Didn't you survive?"

"Yes."

"Was it easy?"

"No."

"Didn't you succeed?"

"I suppose so."

"There's no 'suppose'—you *did*! And you did it independently."

It was very hard for Becky to believe she succeeded. She was stuck in a complicated moment, when she wasn't gaining the acceptance of someone whom others deemed important. And, indeed, George was important in the field of dance.

"You've had disappointment. You want the acceptance of someone who's very powerful. But you're not what he's looking for. That's not to be."

It was a painful moment. She felt she'd failed, especially in the eyes of her mother. That relationship still had a powerful grip on Becky.

"But others did see your power and potential. That's what you need to focus on—the positive. Leave the painful moment in the past."

She was surprised. She thought only her mother and teachers understood this pain.

"Pain is part of life. When something's out of the realm of possibility and clearly not meant to be, we must move on."

"But I did. I had no choice. I had to move on."

"Yes. But the pain of that moment stayed with you. That's not uncommon. However, it's stifled you more than once and led you to make decisions that were not to your advantage. You've allowed yourself to be crippled by *one judgment* that was made by *one person* in that moment in time. And you're reminded of it each time you see your mother. Your perception of her disappointment hurts you more than the actual event. It became a roadblock in your life."

I gave Becky a moment to think about what this meant.

"Your mother isn't disappointed today! But you continue to relive it. You saw how much she sacrificed for you to achieve your dreams and you're embarrassed by the failure. You must let go. You're still trying to impress her. You need to concentrate on what's happening in your life today. Forget what was. You must set new goals. Goals that can be achieved. But you must be willing to think in a completely new way."

"What way is that?"

"Let go of the past. The only thing you need to remember is the passion you felt for your dancing. You must share it in a new way."

She paused to think.

"And my relationship?"

"You're a very strong woman. Why are you spending time worrying about George when you have so much to accomplish for yourself? Don't you want to be independent?"

"Yes."

"Then you must begin by thinking independently. You're too preoccupied with what he's doing. Give yourself mental space to develop your dream. And I'm not speaking of your children. Your family will be fine. I'm referring to your dream of making things better for the next generation of young women like you. Isn't it true that you dream of helping others become great artists? Don't you dream of empowering young women?"

Becky's eyes softened.

"I just don't see how that's possible with all the responsibilities I have."

"Becky, it's time for you to concentrate on yourself. You've been sacrificing too much of what you should be doing for the sake of everyone else. There's a reason why you do that. You were taught a very powerful lesson early in life. Your mother was someone who sacrificed a great deal for her family."

Becky's mother wanted her children to believe she was a very simple woman, but in fact, she was complex. She channeled most of her ambitions through her children and, more than anything, wanted them to succeed. Becky worked very hard to please her mother just as her mother sacrificed a great deal to make sure she got the best education. However, even with these good intentions, parents must remember to lead by example rather than place the burden of success on their child. A child doesn't realize the burden they carry, but the burden is there. The more the mother sacrificed for the child to succeed, the higher the stakes became.

"You must not place the burden of success on your children. Show them how you continue to succeed. Your life isn't over! There's more to do. And your children will be watching with great pride."

"And George?"

"George needs independence as much as you do."

This was sensitive. Becky had sacrificed a great deal for the relationship. She didn't want it to fail.

"George will be a good father. You don't have to worry."

Becky worried that her mother would disapprove of anything that divided the family. And this is what tends to happen: *children perpetuate the mistakes of the parents even when they think there's no comparison.* Just as George was walking in his father's path, Becky was walking in her mother's. In Becky's case it was the devoted-mother path. Her mother had sacrificed her dreams for her family and now Becky was doing the same.

Even though Becky agreed with me, she resisted. It was very difficult to hear what I was saying. It wasn't part of her plan. But I wasn't there to please Becky; I was there to bring out the full potential of *her life.*

She thought about what I said.

"Will I be able to manage on my own?"

"Yes," I answered. I could see that she was going to be very successful in her profession.

"Will the boys be all right?"

"The boys will always be all right. I give you my word."

Becky thanked me, even though she was deeply troubled. I knew we would meet again, when many things in her life would be different.

Eventually, Becky and George separated. It wasn't easy. Many habits and routines changed. They stepped out of their very familiar world and risked dealing with the unknown. They learned a great deal about themselves and approached life with a new set of rules. They understood what motivated previous decisions. They didn't wait to be understood by their partner. The days of blaming each other for their dissatisfaction came to an end. Success or failure was up to them as individuals. They understood the importance of focusing on their goals. They were no longer co-dependent; they were independent.

They became better parents. The time and attention they gave their children was far superior to what it was. They focused on the happiness of the children rather than their own unhappiness. And the children witnessed the happiness born of their parent's achievements. Becky succeeded as a director of several schools. Once she believed in herself, she empowered other young artists. George went on to make the career changes he wanted. He fulfilled his dream of going to college. In addition to having grown as an artist, he also became a very successful teacher. His understanding, patience, and compassion are greatly valued by students and colleagues.

Their children benefited. They were proud of their parent's achievements. They learned great lessons from their very independent parents. *Focus on your dream; do the necessary work and you and those around you will benefit from your success.*

What is the source of your frustration? What is the purpose of your anger? Why punish yourself and others? Answer these questions, concentrate on what's good in your life and put an end to your suffering. Talent and Time must not be wasted. We make a mistake to think we have an infinite amount of both.

PATRICK

Patrick was a man of considerable accomplishment. He believed in dreams. He fought for his. He was also famous.

Patrick was a powerful actor. Many considered him an ideal man. He soon discovered that celebrity is both a blessing and a curse. As in every business, one success needs to be followed by another. The film industry and his admirers expected it, as did he—reasonably or not. The pressure was enormous. But he fought and he believed the pressure made him better. But those pressures inevitably took their toll.

We met at a time when his personal and professional life was cracking at the seams. I felt his suffering despite the brave mask he wore for the public. Fear crept into his dreams; fear of failure in every aspect of his life. Of course, that fear was impossible to recognize because his expectation was always to be the best at everything. He pushed that feeling of fear as far away as he could. He gave it another name—depression. It was a feeling he shared only with his wife, Lisa. His hidden truth came to light without his permission, understanding, or acceptance.

Our story began through George, one of his most trusted friends. George knew Patrick and Lisa were experiencing some difficulties, so he arranged a session with me as a gift.

When I work with a client, I don't see wealth or celebrity. I see a person. Usually, people present themselves in a way that has little to do with who they really are. But when I read them, I see the real person, the person before they learn to pretend. In Patrick's case, the person and his idea of himself were one and the same. From his well-worn cowboy boots to the Stetson on his head, he was a rugged cowboy with the soul of a poet. It was very clear why this charismatic, handsome man was adored by so many. His manner with me was filled with warmth and ease, as though he'd known me his entire life.

He arrived in his mud-spattered Range Rover. Patrick was a cleaned-up version of his rough-terrain vehicle. Like most things in his life, he enjoyed pushing himself and his possessions to their limits. There was nothing precious about this man.

As we drove to their ranch in the San Gabriel Mountains, he asked, "So how do we start this?"

"We've already started."

He nodded.

"Aren't you going to ask me any questions?"

I laughed.

"I don't ask questions. I give answers."

He laughed.

"But I know you don't want me to say anything yet."

"Oh, really?" He asked sarcastically.

"Yes. You want me to wait and say everything in front of your wife."

He gave me a curious smile. What I said was true, but he thought it was a lucky guess. It was certainly no secret that he loved his wife. I could feel how deeply he loved her. I could also feel his pain—emotional pain. It wasn't the right moment to discuss it, so we continued the ride with silly banter.

We arrived at the ranch, his sanctuary from the realities of celebrity. It was a special place. I knew he'd invested a great deal of time into making it special. I could feel that his hands had shaped all aspects of the property. It was made with a lot of love and care.

We were immediately greeted by his menagerie of animals. The dogs were the most excited. His animals loved him as much as he loved them. From the magnificent horses I could see in their stables to the sweet cats that roamed comfortably, they were all precious to him. I could feel the attention and care he gave each animal.

As I tried to step down from his giant SUV, I teased him.

"You know, next time I'm here you should get a little step stool so I can get down without breaking my leg."

"Pretty sure of yourself, aren't ya?" he retorted.

"That's right," I quipped back. "I'm sure of myself."

Lisa came to the front door. She suited him well. She was beautiful, feminine, and rugged at the same time. She gave me a warm, Texas greeting, but I knew she was making an effort. It was not a good day for her. I could feel a profound emptiness. It made me sad even though I'd experienced the same situation a million times before. I would address that emptiness later. For the moment, our introduction was all about keeping up appearances.

I started gently by assessing their environment. It was a rustic, ranch-style home, but many things were in the wrong place. As they well knew, objects have power. We went through the house and I picked a few specific items and explained why they were misplaced. They seemed alternately amused and amazed by my observations. They were particularly impressed when I made some comments in their bedroom. I wanted to help, but I also didn't want to frighten them with too much personal information. It wasn't until we got to their dance studio that it became clear to me why it was time to go deeper.

"There's been entirely too much crying in here."

"Well, it's a dance studio," Lisa said. "A lot of hard work and suffering goes with what we practice."

"That isn't the kind of suffering I'm talking about."

Lisa gave Patrick a glance, as if to ask, "Is she saying what I think she's saying?"

Patrick, ever the defender, jumped right in.

"Dancing can be very frustrating, especially if your body won't do what you ask it to do."

I'm always amazed when people insist on covering up the obvious. I forget that they think it isn't obvious. Too much energy is spent on pretending.

"Okay," I said, "What about that other place where you work?" I pointed toward the basement. "That's not good for you either. You should be above ground. Your place of work needs light. There's too much darkness."

He laughed.

"What's wrong with it? I've done a lot of great work down there."

"Maybe it could've been better. I just know it's not a good place for you."

I could feel and see that it was his place of pain and frustration rather than creation. I chose not to argue. Patience. Timing is everything.

He thought he knew enough about his suffering. He wanted to bypass his workplace and, instead, he wanted to know about their horses. The horses were his joy. I would get to the suffering issue later. We made our way to the stables.

As we walked toward the barn, I turned to him.

"You don't look well."

He gave me a puzzled look.

"I'm fine. Maybe a little tired, but fine."

I had to begin that conversation as soon as possible. I don't always have good news. He wanted to concentrate on his horses. I followed his lead.

The horses were magnificent. I talked about their personalities. They laughed like proud parents. And he continued to test me.

"What kind of horse is this? C'mon. You should know these things, right?"

But I had more important issues to address.

Finally, they showed me their office in the barn. Natural light poured in from the large windows that faced west. The walls were decorated with posters of his films, including the film Lisa directed. I took note of that one because it was a photo of the two of them in a romantic dance pose. He was holding her as she swooned in his arms. It made me sad.

There were two desks on opposite ends of the room, one for Lisa and one for Patrick. A couch and coffee table were in the middle of the room for more casual meetings. I could feel that this was mainly Lisa's workplace. She sat down behind her desk. Patrick sat in a chair next to her and I sat across from them. The sun was beginning to set and the bright light coming through the windows was hitting me directly. He offered to move my chair. But I declined and started with a prediction that would set the tone for the next three hours.

"No. I don't mind the light while I have it. Because," I paused, "soon it's going to get dark."

"Okay, go blind then," he quipped.

"Don't worry." It was time to be serious. "I'll be fine."

I had to address their "performance." They were performing for me. I pointed at Lisa.

"You're sitting right there, but it's like you're not really here."

I turned to Patrick.

"Look at her. She's not here. She's already checked out."

My statement took Lisa completely off guard. She couldn't pretend any longer. She took a quick look at Patrick and turned her head away and began to sob. But I could feel her relief even within the pain. She was grateful I said it. I turned to Patrick.

"You need to look at what she wants, at how to fix this. Because she's out the door."

Patrick looked at her and began to cry. There was so much pain in the room that I was crying as well. The floodgates had been opened. After a few moments, Patrick composed himself and made his way toward Lisa, but her body language was clear—don't touch, fragile.

"It's true. I'm gone. In my heart, I'm gone."

They were in utter despair. The masks had come off. No more pretending. I spoke up.

"Don't you think it's time to talk?"

And we did. We talked a great deal. To quote Patrick from his book, *The Time of My Life*: "[Elizabeth] cut through the bullshit right away."

I revealed several hidden truths for them to see how they arrived at this dangerous emotional crossroad. And I urged them.

"It's better to get things fixed now. Why wait until tomorrow to correct problems that have a solution today? Why not enjoy what we have at this moment? We mustn't waste time with negativity."

They agreed even though they didn't feel my sense of urgency. As with all my clients, their privacy is of utmost importance to me. Patrick's declaration that I saved their marriage must suffice for this part of the story. I could see that their marriage was worth saving. In fact, I knew it was necessary to get it back on a firm footing. Their foundation was crumbling, but I knew their love was true.

However, it was important that I tell them about the other hidden truth, the one I was most concerned about. That was when I saw who Patrick really was. Like all of us, Patrick was far from perfect. But there was much I admired in him. Patrick was a fighter his entire life.

He fought for being true to one's beliefs.

He fought against failure.

He fought against prejudice.

He fought against stereotypes.

He fought against pain and injury.

He fought for his family.

He fought for justice.

He fought for his dreams.

He fought for his marriage.

And he fought me.

He succeeded in every category except one.

Patrick and Lisa made tremendous headway in their marriage after our first consultation. They saw each other differently. They didn't allow negativity to dominate their thoughts. Whenever old bad habits started to resurface, they consciously pushed them back to the dark, depressed place from which they came. They fought hard to forget the past and concentrated on the love they felt for each other. And it showed in their eyes. I was so pleased with their progress.

"Why don't you think about renewing your marriage vows," I proposed.

Patrick's eyes lit up with excitement.

"That's a great idea. We want you to be there."

"And you should prepare to work again."

This was a surprise. He was not expecting any.

"Television. You'll be working in television."

He smiled even though he didn't quite believe me.

"You should also work on a book. This is very important. And you should begin right away."

He had uncanny instinct. He began to resist.

"What's the rush?" he asked.

"There are things you must get done. Like going to the doctor. You've been wasting precious time."

"I don't need to go to the doctor. I feel fine."

"You're not fine. And it's progressing. It's right here."

I placed my hand in an area near my stomach, the problem area.

He argued, insisting that his lack of appetite was a result of worry and depression.

"Now that Lisa and I are good I'm sure I'll feel better."

"It has nothing to do with that."

Finally, Lisa spoke up.

"Why are you arguing with Elizabeth? Why is it so difficult to just follow her advice? I'll make the appointment. What could it hurt?"

I wondered where this man might have been without this practical woman by his side.

"You mustn't procrastinate. No matter what we imagine, we never have as much time as we'd like to have."

I felt his irritation. He was feeling optimistic about his marriage. Work was coming. He was feeling reborn. He was in love again. He had everything to live for. Illness was not on his agenda. He reluctantly promised to do as I asked.

He called after his doctor's visit. I knew he was shaken but, true to form, he fought.

"I know I can beat this."

Unfortunately, I couldn't agree. I didn't say anything.

"You'll see," he said. "I'll win. I've cheated death more than once in my life."

And now I had to be strong—for his sake.

"You don't have forever. You know the type of cancer this is."

He was angry.

"Now we'll never get insurance for the TV series."

The doctors gave him very little time.

"They'll get the insurance, don't worry. You'll be working."

He was stunned when the producers got the go-ahead.

Patrick was such a powerful warrior that he proved the doctors wrong. And me, as well. He would call to tease me.

"I'm still here."

"Yes, you are." I responded with true admiration.

"But get those assignments done."

"You are a true kill-joy."

"The day will come when you'll thank me."

"Can't you just say that I'm going to beat it?"

What could I say?

"I wish I could. But I can't if I don't see it."

He would hang up angrily. It hurt me, but I understood.

Despite these angry exchanges, they would call with questions.

"Would you help us choose an author for the book? Will our horses give birth?" Simple things. And then he would always end by saying,

"I'm still here."

He was a tremendous man. Courageous, funny, and passionate. He fought fiercely for his dreams the way I wish everyone would.

On September 13, 2009, George called me about something or other.

"Oh," I said. "I thought you were calling about Patrick."

"Isn't that funny," he said. "I just got an email from him a few days ago. It said: 'Would love to see you. You're welcome anytime.' I really must get out there."

"Yes," I said. "You'd better hurry. It's time."

Patrick passed away the next morning.

When we flew to Los Angeles to honor the life of this beautiful man, I was pleased to be supported by the arm of Patrick's true friend, George de la Peña. I could feel that George wasn't prepared to let go of his friend, but he attended the tribute nonetheless. I was grateful that George had introduced us and now he escorted me to say goodbye. It was a difficult event for me. Not because of Patrick's passing. In fact, I feel closer to him now than ever before. He's in a place where he no longer must pretend or do things to get applause. He can finally be himself. But the difficulty came from those who were still living. The soundstage where the memorial was held was filled with a lot of anxious people. And it wasn't mourning. It was the anxiety of wanting to look good, look successful. I was glad to be anonymous and not know anyone other than through their fame on screen. I got to know them as I read them. I knew why they were there. I knew what they were thinking about. I knew the purpose of their presence, both positive and negative. I could feel sincerity and hypocrisy. I could feel frustrations and concerns. I could feel fear. Many were suffering the same anxiety: Am I noticed? Do I impress the people who are here? They didn't want to look weak, or old, or tired, or stressed. They were performing for each other. They were covering what they were really feeling. They were all looking for their next great success. Perhaps someone in that room would help them get it, they thought. Such a difficult life.

At the end of the tribute, which Lisa had worked so hard to produce, we all raised a toast to Patrick. I saw him in my mind's eye and said silently, "Now that you can see what's really going on here, aren't you glad you are where you are?"

I could hear his laughter.

You must value yourself. If you allow others to control your life, if you allow circumstances to rule your future, if you believe that your fate has been determined, then you will suffer the consequences of those decisions. You have the power to choose your path. It's up to you whether it will be positive or negative.

HELEN

Late one evening I received a call at our home. It was one of my clients, Helen. I hadn't heard from her in nearly six months. Her voice was barely recognizable. She sounded congested, as though she'd been crying. I looked at the clock on my kitchen wall and calculated the time change in her city. She wasn't in her office as she normally would be at this time of night. Her state of mind was in complete contrast with the luxurious place I sensed she was in, a place that she'd taken me in the past, a place where she recuperated from the stresses of work and life. I could only see bits and pieces of it because her mind was dominated by a dangerous wish. I knew that one of the causes of her suffering at that moment was the man in her life; something I had warned would take place. I also knew that a hidden truth from her past would have a negative impact on both of them. Had she followed my advice, this inevitable revelation would've had a very different effect. Irrespective of my warning, Helen believed that she was financially powerful enough to overcome anything. This belief conflicted with her true nature (she had a gift for nurturing but hadn't learned how to use it) and so her decision to ignore my warning would cost her dearly. On the night she called me, she'd arrived at a point in her life where her past had smashed into her present and the hidden truth that had finally been revealed to her made its full impact. It was more than she could handle.

"I'm sorry to disturb you."

"You're not disturbing me, Helen. I'm always happy to hear from you."

She hesitated.

"I'm calling to apologize and to say thank you. Meeting you was the best thing that ever happened to me. You are the most important person in my life. You and my father."

"You don't sound well. Why don't you tell me what's going on?"

She didn't respond immediately. She didn't need to. I already knew what she was planning.

"I know you've helped me so much in my life. I know that many times I didn't listen. I know I've disappointed you."

"I'm not disappointed in you, Helen. We all must make choices in life and you made yours. I don't judge the people I work with, I just try to help them."

Helen wasn't calling for a consultation. She was calling for a different kind of help—she needed to be held because she was falling apart. Helen had lost the one person she could always rely on when she was in trouble. And there was no one to turn to but herself for the circumstances she found herself in. She was finally at the point in her life where she could see the price of the reckless confidence that her privileged life had given her.

"I just wanted you to know that I love you and that I'm very sorry for not listening. I've behaved very badly with you and I'm ashamed. I needed you to know that before I go."

She paused for a breath.

"After this phone call I'm going to cut my wrists in a warm bath. I don't want to upset anyone anymore."

In that instant, I could see all the people in her life that she claimed she was upsetting, as though a photo album spilled out in front of me. I could have explained many things to her at that moment, things that could've given her some understanding of her circumstances, but Helen was in too much pain to hear anything. All she wanted was to stop the pain. And I, from my home that was hundreds of miles away, had to stop her from what she was determined to do.

I met Helen several years earlier. A mutual friend insisted that I meet her. "Please," my friend pleaded, "she really needs your help."

I agreed to do what I could.

Helen was a very beautiful, sophisticated, and wealthy woman in her early thirties. She dressed modestly for our meeting. When she walked into the room the first thing I read was that she was going to have a child in six months. Her pregnancy was foremost on her mind, but she needed to speak about her husband. I let her speak, something I usually prefer my clients don't do until I've told them what I see. But I sensed that this was a special case and had to be treated differently.

"I'm worried about him. He's always at work. We don't talk anymore. Our daughter rarely sees him. He's making my company a huge success but I'd rather we see more of him than have the richest company in the world. I feel that something is wrong."

I didn't tell her that her concerns were well founded.

"I'm pregnant. I don't want my child to be born fatherless."

"I can assure you that your child will have a father. You want to have a son and you're anxious about that as well. Don't worry. You will have the son you want."

"But I want my children to have a father who is present. Is there something I can do?"

"You must give birth to your child before we do work on other aspects of your life. Have your child, and we'll take care of your other concerns when that's done."

Helen promised to call me immediately after the child was born.

After our meeting, I thought about the privileged environment in which Helen was raised. I saw her surrounded by the finest things one could have. Even so, Helen was missing a critical developmental element in her environment during her upbringing.

Despite this void, Helen developed into an intelligent and well-educated woman. She worked hard and earned the respect of her peers and teachers. When she graduated from college her father gave her two of his established businesses and a substantial amount of money. However, the wealth that she and her family possessed became a source of insecurity for her in the area that would prove to be her greatest challenge—her relationships with men. Helen always doubted the sincerity of the man she was dating. She measured her own self-worth against the lure of her wealth. The source of her ever-present fear of being betrayed was too complicated to explain in our session, but I knew that when the time was right, we would have that conversation.

Helen gave birth six months after our first meeting. She called me.

"I had a boy!"

She was very happy. Helen loved children.

"It's time for you to tell me what you saw. Can you please come to my home? Not just as my consultant but as my guest."

I had plans to be in her city in a couple of weeks, but she insisted that I come immediately. When I arrived and got settled, she asked me to begin our session as soon as possible.

At times, I'm compelled to demonstrate to my clients why they're right to trust my advice. It feels a bit silly, but I know how easily doubt creeps into the mind and so I must remove it by doing something surprising and dramatic.

"Let's go for a ride in your car," I suggested. She was confused by my request but honored it nonetheless. As we drove around the outskirts of her city, I pointed out a large office building.

"Is that building yours?"

"Yes," she responded with complete surprise.

"Let's keep driving." Her story was becoming clearer to me by the minute. A short distance later I pointed to another building.

"And that one? That building is yours as well."

"Yes."

"But you're not allowed inside that building, correct?"

She was so surprised that she could barely speak.

"Yes," she answered.

"Good. Now we can start."

When we returned to her home, we began.

"Your husband is a brilliant and talented man. He's making your company a success. He's also having an affair with his secretary."

Helen blushed with shame.

"This shouldn't be a surprise to you because you already sensed something was wrong when you first came to me. But the affair is less important than what they're planning to do. They're plotting to take your business away from you."

Helen gasped. I knew she was in pain, but I had to move quickly.

"You must take back what's yours."

"But I can't!"

"Are you going to let them take it?"

Silence.

"You must take it back!"

She was afraid of her husband's fierce temper. But, mostly, she was ashamed. She believed she'd failed in business, as a wife, and as a woman. She was focusing on all the things that made her vulnerable. I needed her to focus on fighting back.

"You're going into that building and you'll take back your company."

Helen didn't know what to say.

"You mustn't let a marriage vow stand in the way of justice. Your marriage was finished long ago. We mustn't waste time wondering why it happened. We must move forward. We'll deal with the past when we have things where they rightfully belong. Don't feel remorse for taking back what belongs to you."

Helen's sense of justice was starting to surface.

"You'll also get a divorce."

She retreated.

"He won't give me a divorce. It will be a disgrace for our families. My father will be furious."

The father. That would be a long talk. I would get to him later.

"Everything will be fine. And I'll explain why as we go. Are you willing to fight for what belongs to you?"

Helen agreed.

We began by contacting the employees who were still loyal to Helen and her father. I chose specific names from a list she showed me. She went into the forbidden building and, in little time, had control of her company once again. Her husband was caught completely off guard. He was furious but being a clever man, he soon realized that there was plenty of evidence that we'd amassed against him. There was little he could do but cooperate. He never dreamed that Helen would fight against his wishes.

Helen was finally in her rightful place.

"And now we must get a divorce."

"Elizabeth. He'll never agree to this."

"Not only will he agree, but he'll also agree to any terms you set regarding the children. He'll be a good father to your children despite what's happened."

"But why would he?"

"We all make foolish mistakes, Helen. His mistakes cost him dearly. But he's not a fool. He knows that he has only himself to blame for what happened. He never should've been your husband. But that doesn't mean he doesn't love his children. Have faith—you'll see."

Helen recovered her business and she was no longer under the humiliating cloud of betrayal, deception, and conspiracy. Our success inspired her. She was revitalized and eager to take command of her company.

"I want you to work as my permanent consultant. You've transformed me. I now see that I wasn't taking care of my life. I've always counted on others. I want to show you my gratitude. Please stay with me."

She wasn't quite ready to be on her own. I agreed to return after a much-needed visit with my family.

A few months later, I was back in the forbidden building where Helen was now sitting in her office as the Chief Executive Officer. It was time to focus on her company. I could see that there were employees who were still loyal to her husband and working against Helen. Others were simply not working. We had to clean house. Helen arranged for me to interview everyone and left it to me to decide who was to be let go. I agreed. My objective was to make clear to these disgruntled workers that it was to their benefit to leave.

Unhappiness is not healthy nor is it good in business.

By the end of our meetings, the workers were embracing and thanking me. They all left happily and voluntarily. Except for one. His name was David. He was the only employee that Helen defended.

"Please don't pressure David."

I shuddered when she uttered his name.

"He's had a very difficult time these last few years. He lost all his money. He's in debt. His wife left him. He's a good man. I want to help him. Please don't be harsh with him."

"Are you quite sure you want to do this?"

"Absolutely."

"This man will cost you dearly. Is this what you want?"

"I don't mind losing some money here and there. I have enough to cover it. I want to help him."

"But are you willing to lose everything?"

Helen laughed.

"Elizabeth! Don't be silly. I won't lose everything, especially with you by my side."

Once again Helen was counting on her charmed life rather than seeing what was clearly a losing proposition.

"This is your business to do with what you wish but remember my words: You're making a big mistake if you pursue this man."

She didn't pursue him. He pursued her and she enjoyed it.

David was a very attractive man. He counted on his beauty and charm to get him through life and all its challenges. He was also a man addicted to his pleasures, which included drinking, gambling, and sex. He valued his pleasures more than good, hard work. What made matters worse is that he wasn't suited to the work he was doing in Helen's company. His inability to succeed at work would lead him to satisfying his addictions to have peace of mind—a formula for disaster.

Helen was attracted to David's plight, but she didn't realize that he purposely invested a considerable amount of time to secure his position with her. He used every opportunity to tell her about his difficult life. He described, in detail, the difficulties he'd experienced with his former wife and how she punished him financially. He recounted all his financial setbacks. He presented himself as so ill-fated that it appealed to Helen's compassionate nature. It also appealed to her as a recently divorced woman who'd been betrayed by a man who didn't need her. David portrayed himself as so needy that Helen was sure he would never betray her. She would nurture David. And she felt better about herself consequently. In return, David introduced her to all his pleasures. They began to see each other regularly.

It was at this point that Helen's father contacted me. He heard about what was clandestinely transpiring with his daughter and her employee. He requested a meeting with me. Helen's father was a remarkable businessman and he was completely devoted to her.

"I'm very grateful to you for all that you've done for my daughter. Please continue to be her consultant. Ask any amount, the fee doesn't matter. I want to help her. I love my daughter."

I read him for a long moment, and then I confronted him.

"But you're not being honest with me. You call her 'my daughter' but your wife doesn't."

The man was silent.

"Your wife—the woman in your home—treats her like she's the devil."

He took a moment to compose himself before he responded.

"The truth is," he paused, "Helen is adopted."

I appreciated that he didn't attempt to continue this deception.

"My wife wanted a child, but we weren't able to conceive. I tried to please her by adopting this child. But instead my wife responded with anger. She was suspicious, thinking that it was my illegitimate child. Nothing I explained would calm her. She didn't want Helen. But I wasn't going to take the child back. I'm a man of my word. I adopted her and I wasn't going to shirk my responsibility. I developed a very deep affection for the unfortunate child. But my wife remained cold. As Helen grew, it became clear that I had to make a different arrangement."

The man was a wise judge of character. He knew that his wife would make life miserable for both of them if Helen stayed in the house. He decided to send Helen to a boarding school in order to keep peace in his home. But Helen would forever feel the estrangement even though she put on a brave face.

As he spoke, I thought to myself: Sometimes it's better for children to be sent away from a place that has such strong resentment from one parent. It doesn't change the fact that the child will one day need the love and affection they didn't get from both of their parents.

"I will help Helen," I told him, "because she's going to need it. But you must do your part as well. You can't reward her when she does things that are wrong and bad for her. You must establish limits, or she'll never learn."

"I'll try."

His real belief was that she needed to learn from her own mistakes. Unfortunately, his feelings of guilt regarding the situation led him to protect Helen. Every time something went wrong financially or professionally, he would catch her and break her fall. His heart was in the right place, but he would never give her the kind of guidance she really needed. Helen needed the love of two parents who jointly taught their child right from wrong. It was time to end the session, but I knew I would be hearing from him again soon.

Some months later I got another call from Helen's father.

"I hate to trouble you with such a thing. I hear from friends that Helen is gambling heavily. My contacts say she's losing a lot of money. I realize that I've helped create this situation, but I don't want to embarrass her by putting a stop to it. Could you please help me?"

I noted that he didn't mention David, who was certainly with her. Pride didn't permit him to acknowledge this secret affair. I flew to Las Vegas. When I found her, she was sitting rigidly at one of the gambling tables, paralyzed by her losses. I could feel her distress. She looked like a little toy doll dressed in the most expensive Chanel clothing. As I entered her thoughts, I began to feel what a gambler feels.

"Maybe the next bet will turn things around. Maybe luck will turn back in my direction."

But it wasn't just the loss of money that kept her there. Her dignity wouldn't permit her to leave the table. She was thinking: "I'm wealthy and powerful. I can't leave the table in disgrace."

I gently touched her shoulder. She wasn't surprised when she saw me. It was as though she'd been praying for me to appear.

"And David?"

"I don't know where he is. We had an argument. I think he went to another casino."

I knew he was the one who brought her to this place. It wasn't enough that he was losing money for her company, now he was helping her lose her personal wealth.

"We should go now," I said.

"I can't leave at this moment. One more hand," she stammered.

I decided to wait a little bit longer. As I watched her play, I could see she was playing a role, the role of a winner. But that wasn't going to happen. She continued to lose.

"It's enough now, don't you think?"

She looked up at me with eyes of willful certainty.

"Just one more hand."

I wanted her to stop on her own. It was clear that she couldn't control herself. Finally, I sensed she wanted me to pull her away. I took her by her arm.

"We're leaving now."

She took her remaining chips and we walked away. I could feel her body shaking. She was mortified. Nonetheless, she followed without resistance as I guided her to the hotel elevators. They were gilded gateways for gambling royalty. We entered one that was waiting, and she pressed the button for the penthouse, the exclusive suites for the high rollers. She was thinking: Why would anyone who was truly rich and powerful care about losing money? A truly rich person would always know how to get it back.

When we entered her suite, Helen began to scream uncontrollably.

"You've lost a great deal, but I think we've saved something more important here tonight. We saved you."

Helen called down to the casino and asked how much she owed. I watched her as she wrote down the figure on a piece of hotel stationary, nearly a million dollars. She hung up and screamed with anguish and rage. I went to the bathroom and drew a hot shower for her where she continued to scream in horror and shame. I waited in the living room until she eventually exhausted herself. I watched her as she slept. I saw her as a little girl. I wondered why her father, an intelligent man, didn't see the importance of stopping her sooner. He enabled her. She loved the thrill of winning. He loved pleasing her even when her pleasures were questionable. And, because of his support, Helen believed she was destined to be a winner. He gave her many things, but not the basic tools to survive in the world, like accepting responsibility for one's actions and paying the price.

That day she learned she was an addict. She was addicted to thrill-seeking much like the man she chose. She also learned that she couldn't control everything in her life, especially what she feared most—abandonment.

"We must leave this place and you must never come back."

She assured me that her bad behavior and bad luck was finished. Unfortunately, that wasn't the case.

I tried to prepare Helen for an event that was going to be a severe blow to her mentally, emotionally, and financially. I knew that her father was about to die. She wasn't willing to hear it or believe it. He died within weeks. Not only did she lose the man who protected her throughout her life, but she also lost the man who loved her unconditionally. But this was only the beginning of her emotional upheaval. It was at the reading of his last will and testament that Helen discovered that she was adopted. Helen was devastated. Everything she believed about herself was suddenly not true. Every brilliant attribute of her father was no longer a genetic inheritance. In Helen's mind she was no longer fated to succeed like her father. Instead, she discovered that she was the child of alcoholic parents, who did nothing more than indulge their addictions. Helen chose to believe that these newly discovered parents were, in fact, her genetic inheritance. All the opportunities, all her education, all her accomplishments were suddenly meaningless. She chose to believe in what surely must've been her destiny—failure. As for her mother, it suddenly became clear why the woman she called "mother" had never accepted her. Helen's entire identity was collapsing. And what of her real mother? Why did she abandon Helen? These were questions that Helen decided were not worth answering.

The father left the remains of his fortune to his wife. While he was alive, he gave Helen an enormous amount of wealth. But by this time Helen had squandered most of everything that had been given to her. And David, the man who became her romantic partner, the man I'd predicted would ruin her, was steadfastly by her side. She'd spent her resources feeding and protecting his weaknesses. He never got command of his life and he managed to bring her to his level of existence. Helen's "mother" wasn't interested in supporting their reckless habits. Nor did she admire Helen's determination to help the man in her life. Helen had to make do with the little that was left of her inheritance. This led to a very combative home life. Arguments, alcohol, and depression were now her inheritance. It was from this emotional no-man's land that Helen was calling me to say goodbye.

"Elizabeth, I must go now."

"No, no. You can't leave me like this. Tell me what's been going on."

At that moment, the call-waiting signal on my phone interrupted us.

"Helen, I must take this call, but promise me you won't hang up."

"I've said what I had to say."

"Helen, please! If you love me as you say you do, this is the least you can do for me."

She didn't respond. The call-waiting interrupted again.

"Helen! I must take this call. It could be my son."

She knew that I'd been dealing with a delicate health situation with my son.

"I'll wait."

I quickly switched lines and told the person who was calling to hang on as I grabbed my cell phone. My husband happened to walk in at the same moment.

"Peter! Get on my cell phone and call the Houston police department."

I quickly explained the situation and he immediately called the police. I switched back to Helen.

"I need just another minute. It's my son and he needs my help. Please don't hang up."

By the time I switched phones, Peter had the Houston police on the other line.

"We'd be happy to help you, but Houston has many hotels. If this person happens to tell you where they are please call us back."

I was panicked. I had to get Helen to calm down and focus on the room so that I could identify her location. I got back on the line with her.

"I'm tired of giving," she said.

"And might I add—giving to the wrong man!"

"I'm tired of loving."

"And loving the wrong man! You don't have to live this way. You must stop doing what you're doing. We've discussed this."

"And I'm grateful. But I'm too tired to start over."

"Helen. Would you please pray with me? That's the least you can do after all we've been through together."

She agreed. I began to recite the Lord's Prayer. Her mind got quiet. In that moment, I recognized some things in the room that she was seeing. The table with the razor blade and the pills. The mirror on the wall. The window with the beautiful view of ..." When I finished the prayer, I said, "Why have you chosen that beautiful hotel that I enjoy so much to do this?"

"It reminded me of happy times. I wanted to be in a place where you and I had good times together. That's why I had to call you."

"What was the name of that hotel?"

"What?"

She immediately got suspicious.

"You know I can't tell you that."

But the minute she thought of the name she no longer had to say it. I knew it.

"Helen. My other phone is ringing again. Can you please wait a moment? I need to answer the phone."

She was very suspicious, but she let me go. I got on the phone with the police and gave them the name of the hotel. I also gave them the room number. The police operator was very skeptical.

"If she wants to kill herself, why is she telling you where she's going to do it?"

"This is an emergency. Don't worry about why. Please go there as soon as possible. She's very serious."

I hung up with the police and got back on the other phone with Helen.

"Thank you for waiting."

"Is your son all right?"

"Everything will be fine now."

"I must go then."

"Please don't. We've been through so much together. You can still live a good life. It would be a shame to end it like this."

"I'm tired of being hurt. I'll be the one to inflict the last hurt I'll ever feel."

"Helen! You don't need to do this to stop the hurt. Think of your father who loved you so much. His spirit is looking at you now. He doesn't want you to do this."

"But he's not my father. My father doesn't care."

"The man who treated you like his own child is your father, the man who sacrificed so much for you, the man who didn't abandon you when it would have been more convenient for him to do so. He's the one who cares about what you're going to do with your life."

Suddenly I could hear someone knocking on her door. Helen became nervous.

"Wait one minute, Elizabeth."

She answered the door. The next thing I heard on the phone was, "This is the police. We have everything under control. Thank you very much."

Helen didn't kill herself that day. But sometimes we can go through life as though we're dead. It's a choice. Helen continued her relationship with David. We happened to meet by accident when I was visiting her city. She was no longer wealthy. I saw in her mind that they lived in a very small, humble apartment; far from the luxurious life she once led. David met up with us.

"You see," he said proudly. "You said that we wouldn't last together. But here we are."

"Yes, David. I see. You've won."

"It's not a matter of winning."

"You, of all people, know what I mean."

"We need each other. We're very happy."

"And that's all that matters, isn't it?"

I wished them well and said goodbye.

I watched them as they drove away in their little car. No more limousines for them. I knew that Helen felt comfort with David. But what also stays in her mind is the knowledge that her life would've been very different had she taken charge of it, rather than depending on someone who had no idea of what to do with his own life. And she has only herself to hold responsible for that decision. She abandoned her responsibility to herself. That's true loneliness.

But her story isn't finished. Helen and I will see each other again, even if she doesn't yet see this. There's still hope for a better future. I'm waiting for her call.

Don't defeat yourself. Contamination can come from within. Not feeling at peace with oneself can cause death. It's a kind of death to stay alive yet choose not to really live.

VICTOR

People keep secrets. When they come to me, they're grateful that I can give speech to those buried thoughts. Those secrets can either be buried dreams, longings, feelings of shame, or a combination of all of them. They often keep people from feeling fulfilled. It's difficult for me to observe people who think they have no future, no hope. You must never give up hope. Your hope must be focused on the life that's right for you.

Victor was due at any moment. A woman who'd met me a few weeks earlier at a New York hotel referred him to me. I was giving a talk for some six hundred people. She approached me after the talk because she wanted me to meet with a man she felt was in serious trouble. She wanted to have a relationship with him, but he was "trapped" in another relationship. She loved him and knew he needed guidance. I agreed to meet him and was looking forward to uncovering his story. Unfortunately, I could see that the woman wouldn't experience the result she hoped for.

I was preparing for Victor's arrival when I felt a powerful impulse to go to the bay window that overlooks the driveway up to our house. There he was, right on time, stepping out of his brand-new Mercedes sedan. Victor was a successful business man who had all the trappings of success—wealth, power, assuredness. As I watched him exit his car, I immediately realized why I needed to be at the window. The man I was watching didn't have the body posture of the "successful man" he appeared to be. He slouched from exhaustion, as though he'd been through a war. The battle was over, but he was still fighting. His head was tilted down, his arms hung lifelessly by his sides. His past had a tremendous grip on his present.

As I watched him approach, I observed his past, present, and future. He was three different people.

When he arrived at the door, he intentionally straightened himself, fixed his jacket, pulled on his sleeves, and presented himself in the manner that he thought he should look. He was showing himself in his "present."

After he rang the bell, I opened the door and met his future. He looked like a new person, as though he'd gone through a long journey and had finally arrived. He was even smiling a little, with a feeling of anticipation about what the future might bring. He was also feeling a sense of relief. He'd waited many frustrating years for this face-to-face encounter with the possibility of hope. I knew that I needed to remember all those personalities.

Victor was a man who needed to believe in himself. I was particularly excited at meeting him because I could see his future as bright. I could still feel hope in him, the hope that things could change. He lost hope for his former dreams, but he believed that something about his present could change for the better. He was a good man, but the life he was leading was a lie. Others were making decisions for him. They weren't his decisions. He was fulfilling other people's wishes.

His exterior seemed good, though his heart was lost. He was married, but to the wrong person. He was successful in business, but not at what he wanted to do. He made lots of money, but he had no time to enjoy it. Nor did he believe he would ever have time to enjoy it. He had a big, expensive home, but he chose to live life in one tiny room.

His wife was someone he *had* to marry. Victor was Asian. This is a common cultural practice. She was considerably older than him. Although he felt a great deal of respect and gratitude, he never felt love for her. But he stayed because he felt indebted. Victor had compromised too much of his life.

As I read him, some recurring questions came to me:

- *How can you be committed to someone if you've never committed to yourself?*

- *Why don't we commit to ourselves?*

- *How can you know what someone else needs if you've never permitted yourself the luxury to understand your own needs?*

It was time to speak; we hadn't yet uttered a word. Victor spoke about his home, his past. He talked a little about his immediate family. Their ties used to be so strong and now they'd become so loose. He couldn't remember what was important in his life.

He spoke from his heart for the first time and I responded in-kind.

"Victor, your marriage must end."

He was a bit shocked, but it was a wish deep inside him that he wanted to hear spoken.

"Your marriage isn't really a marriage. It isn't something bonded through love or understanding. It isn't something that's looked upon every day with love and tranquility. It isn't something that either one of you can run to, talk to. It isn't a person who can look into your eyes and, without words, can understand your needs, your feelings. It isn't any of that. I'm sorry."

The truth was overwhelming.

"I not only feel sorry for what's going on in your life, I'm sorry for the time you both have taken from each other. This marriage will soon come to an end."

He was speechless. Finally, he mustered the energy to say something.

"I want to believe what you say but this situation has gone on for such a long time. I can't believe it will ever end."

"Victor, we're talking about *life*." I shook my head side to side. "This has gone on for such a long time. During this period of time you haven't lived."

It was a statement he couldn't deny.

"If you know that everything in life inevitably comes to an end, why don't you also believe that things can begin? How can you not realize or stop and recognize that we must start to live?"

He sat back in a very comfortable position, as though a weight had been lifted from his shoulders. He watched me carefully. He wanted to see how life could change.

"It's time for you to sell your business. You must move out of that line of work."

"I've dreamed of doing that," he said in disbelief.

"Let this also be a part of your past."

Again, he was speechless.

"Let's not talk about what could've been in the past, let's make it happen and then look to the future."

He couldn't see it. But I could, and he needed to believe it was possible, so I had to tell him what I saw.

"Not only will you sell the business, but I'll tell you to whom, when, and for how much."

He deeply wanted to believe what I was saying. I was pleased by the hope and the feeling of love and gratitude he was experiencing. I was finally feeling positive energy from him.

"Tell me exactly what you want me to do so that I can have a chance at life," he said. "This is what I dream. I know what I *don't* want to do anymore. When do I begin?"

"This will all begin in just a few months," I said. I sensed that he was ready to change his life. But he was still unconvinced.

"It's taken you a lifetime to realize that you're not living. Now that you realize this, you don't need to hesitate; you need the strength to move ahead. You must take control of your life! Are you ready? You must not be afraid. You're fighting for yourself, your life, your happiness. You're fighting for whatever's left of your life so that it can be the best."

"But I have financial responsibilities."

"You'll be responsible. I know how you are. Be warned that this will not be simple. This will be a costly divorce."

He smiled. He liked that I was referring to the divorce as though it was already in progress. He suddenly got lighter. He was beginning to believe in my vision. The consultation ended. I could feel his excitement. He thanked me and asked when he could come back.

"Very soon."

He beamed with joy.

"I feel so different, so much better. I'm okay with going to work today and tomorrow. It's okay because I know my unhappiness will finally end."

He walked faster when he left. He could barely contain himself. His happiness became my happiness.

It doesn't happen like this with everyone, but he was willing and open.

Today, Victor is a very thoughtful man who believes that circumstances in life can really change. Life is filled with one miracle after another.

Happiness is not just given to us. We must believe we deserve it. If we don't have it, we must find it. Happiness isn't based on the material things we have, it's based on knowing who you are and feeling good about yourself. Happiness should not be based on the size of your home, especially if you find yourself hidden in just one of those rooms. Happiness will elude you if you don't have the right companion to share your feelings.

The goal for life, at the end, after so much hard work, should be simple and peaceful. Life comes to us empty, and it's up to us to fill it. We fill it with hopes, dreams, and wishes. That's the task of a fulfilling life.

Victor believed he needed an opportunity to change his life. He got that opportunity. He also needed to be honest with his companion so that she could also find a new beginning. He learned to address the people who didn't notice his pain, the people who only wanted to criticize his decisions. He decided to go ahead and dream, and to act to make those dreams come true.

Victor moved out of the big house and gave up the fancy car. He now lives in a small apartment and has time for a few friends. He lives life one day at a time. Victor's finally found himself. He can now look into a mirror and really like what he sees. Victor makes time to meditate about life, which is something he never did. He thinks about his emotions—happiness, sadness, and loneliness. They're all part of life. But they're his emotions. He's living his life, not the life that he felt obligated to live. Victor is a much happier man.

Live life with full awareness. Yes, evil exists. But there's also goodness. There's also the hope of tomorrow.

TIMMY

Sometimes in our desire to protect our name and our family, we deny the truth and, consequently, risk hurting the innocent.

A good friend and client of mine, who is also a psychologist, called me. He had clients that were having an unusual problem with their little boy. Timmy was about six years old. He inexplicably, and suddenly, stopped talking. The doctor was at a loss and asked for my help.

"I've met with the boy and his parents both together and separately. The boy sits there and won't talk. He doesn't respond to questions and he's not eating. The parents have no idea what precipitated this behavior and they're getting very worried. They've tried everything—his favorite foods, toys, you name it. He barely responds and it's never with words. The parents thought something might've happened at school. They came up with nothing. Now they're counting on me. I've tried everything to communicate with him, but nothing is working. Would you help me with this?"

"You know that I can't do this unless I have the parents' approval."

"I've spoken to them about you. They don't believe in any of this, you know," he said, "but they're so desperate they're willing to try anything."

So, I met the mother and father at his office. They were in their thirties and clearly very well-to-do. It was also clear that they were suffering with worry. On top of that, there was added concern that I might "do" something to their child. They wanted to know if I intended to use anything on him, was he going to remember what I did.

"I'm not going to do anything. I'm going to talk to him."

"You can't talk to him. He doesn't talk!"

"He doesn't talk? He's never spoken?"

"No, no. He did talk. But he hasn't said anything for almost a month now. We've gone to every doctor. There's nothing wrong with his throat. He hasn't been left alone. Nothing's been different in his life. Everything's the same!"

I listened calmly. They were frightened.

"Anything you can do we'd really appreciate."

My client, the doctor, pulled me aside and said, "He always walks with his little Teddy bear. This has now been his fifth visit."

"What have you gained in this fifth visit?"

"Nothing."

Then he turned to the parents and said, "I want you to understand that Elizabeth will be reading his mind."

The mother responded, "Reading his mind?"

She was surprised and somewhat irritated.

"What's there to read in the mind of a six-year-old? What could a six-year-old be thinking?"

"He would be thinking about what's important to him. Obviously, he's just not able to communicate those things with you right now."

"He's a very loving child. He tells me everything. He's very happy! And suddenly, it just stopped! It had to have been something that happened at school. But I've been to the school. I've asked all the questions. I've done everything that I can. But there's nothing. And he won't talk about it! We've asked every-one—his friends, family, everyone."

"When did this happen?"

"It started on a Wednesday. Timmy went to school that day and everything seemed fine. He was involved in rehearsals for a play at school and had been studying his lines very hard."

"But he did really well," the father said. "He waved to us after the play."

"He seemed really happy," his mother continued. "We didn't suspect that something might've gone wrong during the per-formance until later. We thought maybe he'd forgotten some-thing or missed a cue, but everyone we spoke with agreed that it went well. I remembered later that he wouldn't talk on the telephone that night. But he went to school the next day as usual. Everything seemed normal until we got a call from his teacher. Timmy was not responding to anyone. He just sat in his chair. The teachers would ask him a question and he just wouldn't respond. They called us and said that he needed to go home because something was obviously wrong. We took him to our doctor because we thought that maybe he couldn't describe a pain he was having. Outside of not talking, our doctor couldn't find anything wrong with him."

But she knew something was very wrong. Timmy didn't have any light in his eyes. There was no excitement like I knew there had been.

"He doesn't even smile."

She wanted to cry. The father spoke up.

"Maybe I was supposed to do something with him, and I forgot," he offered, trying to take the blame.

"We did go on occasional trips without him and I know he really wanted to go with us, but we would always bring him a gift afterward and he seemed okay with that. What I'm saying is that it wasn't the first time or anything like that. He's never alone; we leave him with family always. Everybody loves him. It's never been a problem before."

"Is he punishing us," asked the father. "He's acting like he's punishing us."

I knew they were giving me as much background as they *wanted* to give me. There was an important piece of information they were omitting. It was a truth that they couldn't even imagine. But I couldn't let this suffering go on.

"I'll do the best I can."

It was time to meet Timmy. I asked them to be with me in the room when I went in because I didn't want the boy to feel separated from his family.

Timmy was sitting on the couch clutching his Teddy bear. The mother introduced me.

"Elizabeth is my friend. I know you don't know her but she's from New York and she's worried about how you're feeling so she's going to be in the room with all of us while the doctor is talking to you."

The boy didn't blink. He was there but he wasn't listening to anything anyone was saying. The doctor began the session.

"Timmy, I'm going to ask you some questions and then maybe Elizabeth will ask you something, okay?"

The boy didn't respond.

"Is there anything hurting you or bothering you?"

There was no reaction. He just sat holding his Teddy bear. It was a worn little brown bear about twelve inches long. It was all I really needed to see. I knew that everything that Timmy couldn't tell us, he'd told to this worn little Teddy bear.

"Can I speak now?"

"Of course, Elizabeth, please do."

"Timmy, can I hold your Teddy bear," I asked gently.

He didn't look at me. He just handed the bear to me. Perhaps it was because I didn't ask him about what was hurting him. I asked for something that was outside of him. Timmy's mother was amazed.

"You know, Timmy, this reminds me of my son's Teddy bear when he was your age. It's not the same of course, but this one's really nice."

I knew he was listening.

"You don't want to talk," I said, supporting his decision. "You could, but you don't want to. I tell you what, why don't you think about what's bothering you. Think about what's hurting you. Think about what you don't want to think about. Think about what's making you sad or anything that any one of us may have done to upset you."

He started to remember, and I began to see what happened. It will be hard for some to understand what I felt at that moment, but it's the way I saw it. I felt sorry for the person that hurt Timmy. You see, it may have brought him confusing satisfaction in the moment, but once he'd come to an understanding of himself and his actions, he couldn't live with what he'd done.

The problem with innocence is precisely that—innocence. You can't expect a child to express something they don't understand. You and I come to that understanding through education or experience. The child doesn't yet know that there are certain things that we adults consider to be bad. And we adults are too embarrassed to expose their innocent minds to those bad behaviors.

What happened to Timmy happened with a person whom he trusted, whom they all trusted. It happened in a way that was unacceptable to the child because children can't think that way. In Timmy's mind, a person he loved and who he thought loved him, loved Timmy in a way that hurt him. It caused a problem for the person who did it, too. It was his uncle, his father's brother. But it didn't hurt him in the same way. His illness is that his satisfaction comes first and then his pain comes later.

Timmy didn't know how to express what he was feeling. We know it to be traumatic, but to Timmy it just happened. There are no words in the vocabulary of a six-year-old to express what he'd gone through. Therefore, it was better not to speak at all.

We, as parents, sometimes ask questions according to how we see things. But if we think of the child who's the victim, and he doesn't understand he's become a victim, they don't know how to answer. We could ask:

"Has anyone done something wrong to you?"

How could something that a loved one does be considered wrong in the eyes of a child? How could someone who loves you do something wrong to you?

"Did they spank you?"

"No. He didn't spank me."

"Did they hurt you?"

"No."

We could bombard him with questions that *we* understand but he doesn't. So rather than shout out what occurred, he sat silent because he couldn't answer those questions. So, I spoke for him.

"It's going to be okay, Timmy. It's okay. It's not your fault. It's okay to tell mommy and daddy that uncle touched you." I used the Teddy bear to illustrate. "It's okay to tell them that he touched you here," I pointed at the bear, "and there ... and there. It's okay to tell them you don't want to talk because you don't want it to happen again."

I paused.

"Does it still hurt you, Timmy?"

He didn't look at me, he looked at his mother. The mother was in tears. She didn't want to understand, she didn't want to believe. But she could see that I'd gotten Timmy to a point of trust where he was reacting even though he wasn't ready to speak.

When people can't speak, sometimes they prove their innocence and sometimes they prove their guilt. At that moment, as I held Timmy with the Teddy bear, I became speechless. I could feel that Timmy wanted to yell but he couldn't. Tears fell out of his eyes, but he couldn't yell. He needed to be held by arms he could trust.

The world is not the place we pretend it to be to our children. There's good and bad everywhere. You can't trust yourself or a child to anyone. The parents had taken a trip that they'd taken many times. They left him with the family. It had always been fine in the past. But this time the uncle couldn't control himself. He told Timmy that he loved him. They would share a secret that they must keep to themselves. He wasn't allowed to tell anyone. Timmy didn't understand what love meant at that time. He didn't find pleasure in what his uncle described. He did understand the request not to tell anyone. That's why Timmy kept his silence.

I held him and told him it was okay to tell mommy and daddy. I promised him that it would never happen again.

"It's important to tell mommy and daddy even though uncle said not to."

"Look at me, Timmy," I said firmly. "I promise you, nothing like this will ever happen again. But you've got to tell mommy and daddy because I know it's true."

It seemed to him that I knew everything. I made it easy for him by describing the events that he kept secret.

He opened his arms and reached for his mother. She came over, tears streaming down her face, and held him in her arms. She told him that she loved him and that she was so sorry for what happened.

"I love you, too, mommy," he cried softly.

I went out of the room because I was no longer needed there. The father followed me out. He pulled on my jacket.

"What do I do now?"

This is the saddest part of the story. This is why things continue to repeat themselves. I felt such anger.

"You know that this isn't the first time this has happened." He was speechless. "But it's the first time it's happened to someone you love."

He was very upset. He talked about his mother and father and how they loved his brother. They didn't know what to do.

"Now that this has happened to your son, do you still love and care about your brother the way you used to? Has your love changed now that he's changed someone you love?"

He didn't have to answer.

People want to cover up problems. They don't understand the pain this "problem" can bring to other people. So, they cover it up until *they* start feeling the pain. For some, the family name is more important than the obligation to protect innocent people. This could've been avoided if they'd dealt with this unpleasant truth rather than pretend it would go away. It had happened other times. They were able to protect themselves from litigation; they were able to make excuses for the ill brother. "It's not his fault. It's somebody else's fault."

Timmy paid the price for this stubborn deception. And now Timmy is the living victim who will forever remind them of the brother's psychological illness.

Sometimes we're very busy. We want to get things done. We put a lot of faith in others, even though we know there's something wrong. But we don't want to imagine the worst. We don't believe it's possible. So, we take a risk. We can take risks with ourselves. We should. But not with young innocents who can't protect themselves.

The father wanted to pay me for doing a good job. I didn't want his money. This was a painful consultation. It was also painful to understand that this man never would've considered speaking to me had this incident not occurred. He certainly didn't believe that readings like this are possible. But now he believes. It's sad that his son had to be the sacrifice that taught him this painful lesson. Someone else's hidden truth is now and forever part of Timmy.

Be true to your nature. Living life for some may be difficult. Imagine what it must be like to live two lives. Don't alienate yourself from your true self. There's a place for everyone.

JOHN

ohn was born and raised in the American Midwest. Students referred me to him from a university where he taught. When we spoke on the phone, I could sense that he was a very special, very good person. He was excited to meet me. He was quite nervous. He was carrying a heavy emotional burden.

It was a very snowy day. I sat in my hotel room watching the blizzard from my window thinking that whoever had the strength to brave this weather probably needs my help. My phone rang and John was that person. He arrived for his consultation.

A few moments later, there was a strong knock at the door. It was full of caution. A man in his late thirties entered. I immediately felt John's outstanding intelligence. He was distinguished, elegant, and had the chiseled features of the film actor Christopher Reeve. He had striking blue eyes, dark hair, and I noticed that he wore a wedding band. But there was something about his look that unsettled me. After we greeted each other, he took off his raincoat and boots. He wore a big, bulky sweater that had pockets in the front. He kept one hand buried in one of those pockets.

"I almost didn't make it," he laughed.

"That's just like you, John," I responded. "It seems to be a part of your life." He was surprised by my statement but decided not to question it. He didn't realize that the session had already begun.

"Is there anything I need to say?" he asked.

"No. You really don't have to say anything. But if there's something you wish to ask about me, feel free."

"It seems very surprising to me that I would come to see you and that the people that recommended you to me know nothing about me; not that much anyway. Then, on top of that, you tell me that I don't have to tell you anything about me."

"Ask me."

"What shall I ask?"

"Ask anything that will make you comfortable with my presence and with who I am."

He paused to think.

"I just want to ask you—why is life full of desires?"

"Without desire there's no reason to live. Once we lose desire, we lose everything."

He thought a moment and then cautiously continued.

"Is it fair to have desires at any time of your life? Even when your life seems complete and your dreams seem to be on track?"

"It's part of life. It's important to live with desire and dreams."

He seemed confused by this answer. He also didn't understand the protocol for how to begin our session, which, as I said, had already begun. He had a different image in his mind as to how "these things" are done.

"Is there anything I *have* to say, anything you want me to write down?"

"Nothing."

As I looked at John, I began to piece together a very complex puzzle. I saw a woman behind him. Let me explain—these are *my* visions. They're literal for me. John had walked in with a woman very close to him.

"You seem to have a woman companion who doesn't leave your side."

He tried to be very matter-of-fact.

"Well, I'm married."

"No. It's not your wife."

He searched for a possible answer.

"I recently lost an aunt whom I loved."

"No, it's not your aunt."

He waited a moment to see where I might go with this.

"Go on. Don't stop," he encouraged.

I stood up from my chair and walked around him a few times trying to understand the things I was seeing, trying to understand *why* I saw the images that I saw. I asked myself, why would a man who seemed so passionate about life ask me about desire?

From one angle I saw so much anger. From another, so much fear. And when I faced him directly, I saw confusion. I didn't know what to think. I was surprised by the change in John's personality and by the person who now started to appear before my eyes.

"Enlighten me with your vision," he asked eagerly.

I smiled. "Yes, I'll definitely enlighten you."

He was thinking about his family.

"I can certainly help you with your son, your wife, and your career."

"Anything else?"

"Yes, I'd like to talk to you about *you* and everything that I see. There's an image that appears every time I focus on you."

"My son?"

"Not your son, although he seems to be doing well. He seems confident. He appears to know what he wants at his young age. And he seems to get what he needs and wants all the time."

"My son is very special. Of course, most of the parents who I talk to think their children are special."

"Your son certainly is special. He has all the love he could wish for from you and even more."

"What do you mean by 'even more'?"

"The way you love him. The *way* you love him," I repeated, giving emphasis to his generosity of spirit.

"I guess it's very important that we give our children what we've found lacking in our own childhood."

I paused.

"You accept everything he does so well."

John explained his reasoning.

"Well, he does things properly. I encourage him to play baseball, to run, to swim, to believe that he can do and be anything he wants to be."

I smiled when he made this statement.

"That doesn't seem like *your* life, John. It doesn't seem like you've been given the opportunities that you're giving to your son."

"But isn't that the purpose of life—to give our children more than we ever had?"

"Yes," I answered, wishing he could hear his own words. But it was time to focus on another important part of his life.

"Your wife—she seems to have been ill. She's doing better now."

"Yes," he said with genuine care.

But he didn't realize something else about her.

"She's worried about you, John."

He chose not to understand.

"I don't know why. I feel healthy as an ox."

"Ox?" I asked, showing him that I was surprised by this comparison.

"Yes. I'm a very healthy man."

I needed him to begin to understand that I knew he was hiding something that had little to do with a physically fit person.

"Are we referring to a healthy mind, or only a healthy body?"

"Why? Do you see anything I don't see? Do you see an illness? Suffering? Something I should worry about?"

"Not really. It's not an illness. But, you know, you shouldn't worry about the things you suffer."

He was beginning to get nervous.

"I'm a little ..." he paused. "Confused."

"Why, John?"

"Because I don't feel that I have problems. I come to you because I need to know more about my work, my career, to know if we're moving, to know the things that others say you know so well."

I was getting closer to the reason why he'd come to me. He was nervous but also excited.

"Why is it that I feel you have a desire to hide?"

He pretended not to understand.

"Why would I want to hide?"

"I don't know. I can't seem to tell from the outside. I must ask your permission to look as deep as I can. I need to make the connection between the woman who you came in with and with what you're hiding."

I paused for him to think about what I said.

"You seem to be a man who's quite sensitive. You seem quite enthusiastic about life. But you don't seem happy."

"Doesn't everyone have something to complain about?

"You know there are certain words or statements that I make to people. To some people I use it as a statement, to others I use it as a description of who they are."

I needed him to let go of his fear.

"I wonder: In this life—have you lived? Or have you always just existed?"

"Elizabeth, I've traveled all over the world. I've achieved the career that I worked so hard to get. I'm married with a child. My mother has passed away, my father is still alive. I'm responsible as a husband and as my parents' son. I'm responsible as a brother and as a friend. Why do you see something not right? What do you seem to understand from my question about desire?"

"First of all, in this room, anything that happens, any conversation, stays between us. Who you are, where you're from, what you do are not important to me. When you leave, you will be a memory. And I hope a success story."

"What do you mean a success story? If you were to look at the American dream, I'm already a success story. I own two cars, paying off a mortgage on a very large, beautiful house, and I have a prestigious title in the career I've wanted all my life. I have a beautiful wife and son. What more is there?"

"Do you have yourself, John?"

I paused for him to consider the question.

"Do you have the desire in life to go on? Why is it that when I see you, it's as though part of you has died? It's as though you have a life-threatening illness and you're just waiting for this illness to take over. Why is it that I see you as being so caring to everything and everyone around you, and yet there seems to be a part of you I don't understand?"

I paused again. Sometimes I like to give my client the opportunity to consider revealing what they've been hiding. I had to be very careful with what I was about to say.

"Maybe it's worth looking into. Maybe your desire is something unconscious. You know, desire can change life for the better once we discover what it is."

He was surprised by this.

"Discover? Do you think there's something about myself I don't know?"

"No, John. But there's nothing about you that I don't know as well."

He laughed loudly. And then the blood drained from his face. He looked at me with great intensity. His eyes were searching through me. They seemed to shake with fear. He seemed to be happy with what he hoped I would say, but, at the same time, there was fear. I decided to give him a little more time.

"John, are you planning a trip?"

Again, he was surprised.

"Yes, I'm planning a trip. I like to travel ... as I said before."

I paused.

"Are you going with your family or are you going alone?"

"Alone."

He got nervous again.

"I think I'm going to take a short vacation on my own."

"On your own? Really? By yourself?"

"Why? Do you think I have a mistress?'

I smiled inwardly.

"No. That's not what I'm concerned about."

I could feel his increasing nervous excitement.

"I'm concerned about the intention of your trip. If you'll be able to live out your desires or even fulfill your desires during the period of this trip. I want to tell you something, John." He smiled at me. "At this point, let me just tell you something about yourself that I think is very important that you know. First, I don't really believe you're living. You're existing. You're not being true to yourself. Second, I believe you're circling around society. You live in this society, and you're looking for the approval of this society, but you don't seem to understand or accept your personal desires unless the people around you approve them. So, because of these things in your life, you know you'll never find approval here. Is that why you're going on your trip?"

He stared at me, dazed. He put his hands in his sweater pockets and closed one fist around the object he kept with him at all times. We were quiet, so quiet we could hear the wind whistling in the trees outside. John was sweating even though it was mild in the room. It was an ironic contrast to the wind and snow outside. He was sweating because he was coming face-to-face with what he'd been trying to hide for such a long time.

I pondered how to tell him. I tried to plan a way whereby I could explain, and he could understand how I see the things that I see. His methods, his behavior, and his intentions all fought against his true desires. He deflected. He decided to change the topic of conversation even though he wanted so much to hear what I was about to say. He wanted assurances on other matters first. He pulled out his wallet and showed me a picture of his son.

"This is my son. Do you have anything to say about him? Is there anything I should be concerned about?"

I looked at the photo.

"My goodness, John, this boy looks just like you. So very similar to his father."

"Thank you. I'm so proud of him."

"Are you worried about him?"

"Worried? Why? Should I be?"

"Are you worried about what he would do if you weren't here?"

"I've taken care of that."

He wanted to show me how practical he was, but I was referring to something else.

"He already experienced his grandma dying. He knows what death is about. Insurance papers have been put in order. He won't need anything should anything happen to me."

"I'm not talking about death. I'm talking about you needing to go away, far from your son. Have you left enough memories in your son's mind to cover your absence?"

"I don't think I'm going anywhere."

"John," I insisted, "have you done enough with him so that he can remember you when you're not here?"

"I really don't understand why you're saying this!" He was getting quite upset. "Should I see a doctor?"

"John, can I please be open? Can you please be fair with me?"

"I want to hear what you have to say only because I want to know how this will end. But I also don't want to hear what you have to say," he stammered, "because of the pain it will cause the people whom I love so much."

"That pain can be taken away. You must understand that when I walk into a room or I walk into a person's life, I let go of every prejudice. Nothing that has to do with my personal beliefs is involved at this moment. What I see is *you* and what *you* represent, what kind of a man you are and have been and how the world will remember you."

He was clutching the object in his sweater. I was trying to understand how the object in his pocket gave him enough strength to go on with our conversation. How was it able to make it easier for him to accept what I had to say? It wasn't a picture of his son. So, I asked him, "What do you have there?"

He deflected.

"Maybe if I show you a picture of my wife you'll see. Maybe you'll tell me more about her."

I didn't repeat my request because I knew he didn't want to answer my question. So, he pulled out a picture of his wife. I read her. She was a beautiful woman, a kind and understanding woman, a loving woman.

"Will she be okay?"

"I don't see anything wrong with her."

"Are you sure she'll be okay?"

"She'll be fine." And then I added with emphasis, "she'll understand."

This upset him.

"No! I mean her health. Does she seem fragile? Is there anything wrong? Is there anything I need to prepare for?"

"No." And then I looked at him squarely and said, "You've been preparing for a long time, a very long time. But I know that the death of your mother brought out a lot of difficult feelings for you."

"She was special. Could that be what you see behind me? Could that woman be my mother? You know, she always guided me and loved me so much."

"No, it's not your mother. Your mother is present, but that's not her."

He was really getting alarmed.

"But how do you know?"

"Just trust that I know."

We paused.

"Ever since she died, life has been very difficult. It's been one difficult day after another. We were very close."

"I can feel it."

"She understood me."

"Yes! I know."

"I was her only son."

"Yes."

"There's a bond between a mother and son. You know that."

"Yes, there's a bond. And there's also an understanding, a friendship between parent and child. Not for everyone. But some are lucky enough to receive unconditional love that no one else can offer. You must remember: We're all just human beings; we see things *our* way."

"You sound just like her."

"I don't mean to sound like her. I mean to let you know that I know what she's saying."

There was sadness in his eyes. He was missing his mother.

"She says she loves you and she understands. And she's very sorry for not being able to understand things before. But you were such a good boy. You spent most of your life just doing what people expected of you, *when* they expected it of you, and *how* they expected it of you. But you know John, right and wrong are just options in our life. Just options. At times, criticizing our circumstances is a method for coping. Our behavior is what brings out who we are."

He seemed to understand this. And then I went deeper.

"Therefore, accepting what you're *not* is unfair to yourself."

"What do you mean accepting what I'm not? I know what I am! I've worked very hard to get where I am today."

"Really, John? Is that because you wanted to or was it to please others, to find acceptance from others? Because accepting yourself has not been that easy?" I paused. "I don't understand how you can love your son and your wife so much, which I know you really do, and not love yourself as well."

"I've learned. I've been loved too."

"The most important thing in life has to be accepting your-self as you really are."

"I am the person I have to be."

"No. That's not what I said. You're a very successful academic man, a wonderful husband, and a very loving father. But in all of that, I don't see what you are to yourself. Why is it that you can give so much to the world and so little to yourself?"

"Well, I learned a long, long time ago: If you don't do things right, you don't get a reward."

"And what do you mean by that?"

"Will I walk out of here as I walked in?"

"No one ever does. I don't think you will either."

"Elizabeth, can you please just tell me what I need to know?"

"What you need to know is what you've forgotten. You've kept it hidden in the back of your mind. You only live with the desire, not the idea that it can become a reality."

We paused for him to reflect.

"Now that my mother is no longer here, I won't be hurting her. My father never really cared so it doesn't really matter which way I go. But the people who've loved me and I've loved so much, what will happen to them?"

"What you mean to ask is, what will happen to them if they find out, or get to know that inside of you lives another human being who's yearning to come out, who's given everything but has never felt he's received, who's lived his life like a performer, one performance after another, looking for applause after his successful pretending. Is he hoping that people will be able to accept him as he pretends to be so that he can take his bow and move on to the next day, the next week, the next year?"

The pretending needed to come to an end.

"John, shall I tell you what you're holding in your hand?"

"No! Not yet."

He was feeling like a prisoner of thirty years afraid to go out in society.

"But I would appreciate you telling me why?"

"You're such a loving person. Currently of your life you're such a loving man. What you feel inside is no one's fault. What *you* feel is only being suffered by *you*. What can I say? You're planning on going on this trip and maybe never returning. You should learn to accept yourself as you really are. Everything that you've done in your life, to the people around you, and to the people whom you love so much, they'll always remember your love. And at times in life when we must gamble to discover true happiness, we must find out if we've done enough for the lives of others. This entitles us to move on with our own lives. She loves you and she'll always love you. Will she blame herself? She will be confused—very confused. It's been many years that you've been able to perform this way."

He was crying inside.

"Before your mother's death, because you loved her so much, you held back. You held back so much. You didn't want to be a disappointment in her life. And now that she's gone, now that she's no longer here, part of you wants to be free. But then there's another part of you that's holding off. It's because of the love you have for the people in your life and for the son you've brought into this world."

He suddenly became very embarrassed. He pleaded with me.

"You have to understand."

He began to cry openly.

"Please understand, Elizabeth."

"I do. I know that this is something that lives inside you. I know that this is something that you were born with. I know this is something that really *is* you. Your mother and father worked very hard to change your attitude, your personality, your frame of mind, your way of thinking. You changed who you were because you wanted to obey. There comes a time in life when we must face ourselves and ask: Have I been fair to myself? How much can we care about the world and not know how to care about ourselves? Let me tell you what you're holding in your hand."

"I'm ashamed right now, Elizabeth! Please let's not talk about it."

"How can I not talk about who you are? How can I not help you to walk out of this room a free human being? How can I not see inside of you the wonderful man you've been? And the things you've done for others! You stripped yourself of your truth, the person who you really are, and became what others felt you needed to be. And why? You've lived this life and now, suddenly, after thirty-seven years ... what? Will they criticize you? The world always criticizes. Will they be angry? Of course. Will you ever get to see them as you go on your true journey?

Will they try to understand what you're trying to say? It'll take time. But it's better than living a lie."

I waited.

"I know what you're going to do once you leave this room. You're going to go where you have that locker and you'll spend maybe an hour or two there. And after you spend that hour or two, you'll take a bow and then go on to play your other role, your next performance. You'll go home and you'll be a loving father, a loving husband. You'll close your eyes and try to sleep. But you'll feel turmoil, anger, and tears in your dreams. How can I ask you to go on this way the rest of your life? You need to set yourself free! Because that woman I see behind you is *you*. It's just you."

He gasped.

"Elizabeth, why do you say that? How do you know?"

And then he gave in. He pleaded. He was desperate.

"What am I going to do? Sometimes I feel that death is the best thing for me."

"Why? Why do you need to talk this way? Why is it that you don't understand? You feel you must walk away from life. You must walk away from the life you no longer want to live and allow yourself to live the life you're looking for, you're yearning for, you're living for, you're crying for, you're dreaming for. In this amazing and complex world, you'll be surprised; there are some people who will understand you. Just like me."

I paused.

"Your son? Oh, he loves you so much. And you love him back. Your wife? Believe me, John, there's something that she suspects, something that won't surprise her when you share it with her. Be gentle with your words. Don't allow her to blame herself for the things that you've suffered way before she came into your life."

He was overwhelmed with emotion.

"Oh, I feel so free! I want to cry, I want to laugh, I want to jump, I want to run, I want to hide."

He paused.

"I want to die."

I comforted him.

"No. You can't say all those wonderful things that you want to do and in the same breath mention death. Because after all the love that you've given them, they will understand. They will accept."

"Now, I know you have a locker and that locker is full of women's clothing. And in your right hand you're holding a woman's garment. You're holding a pair of women's underwear."

"Elizabeth! Please! If anyone knew ..."

"John, listen to me! Your story lives in many people. I've met others like you, and I'll meet more. But all I want is for you to be free. To love yourself the way you deserve."

He was embarrassed. He needed to explain something.

"I don't want to be with a man! It's not that type of thing."

"I'm not asking you *what* you want to do."

"I just want to be me. I just ... I just ... would like to be me."

"I'm not here to judge you. I'm not here to tell you which way to go or why to do it."

He kept apologizing for who he was.

"I believe in God."

"And he believes in you. You do what's best. But make sure you don't lie to others and don't lie to yourself. And what's left of your life, live it with honor, with respect, with dignity. Don't die. Don't let yourself die!"

He began to weep again.

"Elizabeth, why do I feel you're my mother at this moment? Not the mother that I had, just a mother, a woman who can talk to me, who can explain to me."

"I don't know. I don't know what it is you want to see. But you need to go home, you need to share with your family, you need to give them all the love you have and I'm sure they'll understand. But what you can't do is live a lie. You can't continue to hurt and take the time of others because, maybe today you decided to stay with them, but those days will end. I think you've decided this many times. If you don't leave them today or tomorrow, you'll certainly leave them someday. I'm sure. I just want you to know that no matter what you do in life, you must be fair to others and be fair to yourself. So ... the woman with you is you."

"Elizabeth, this is what I dream. This is what I hope. Can I show you something? A picture?"

"Of course."

He pulled out a photo.

"Look at this."

The tears were streaming down his face. It was a picture of a woman.

"She understands."

"I understand."

"No! She really understands. Do you see who this is?"

"Yes, I see."

"Elizabeth, this is me!"

He walked around the room. He said things that he needed to say.

"But why is it that I still love my wife and my son?"

"They're a part of your life, a part of your life that, no matter what happens, you'll never forget them, and you'll never stop loving them, no matter what!"

John embraced me. He held me for a long emotional moment. I could feel the joy in his heart. I felt his gratitude in his gentle embrace. He was a changed person. When he was ready, he gathered his things and departed. The truth had set him free. As I looked through my hotel window, I saw John entering his car. He was no longer two people. He was finally one with himself.

We must be open to change. Change will open what seems closed in our lives. Courage comes to those who don't fear change.

MICHAEL

Michael is a devoted family man. He's also a problem solver. Whether it concerns his mother, father, wife, in-laws, children, or all of them together, he always keeps them and their needs foremost in his mind. He's also a very organized and successful engineer. He's a realist. He's a man who sees a task, plans, and executes it for a successful resolution. Like most mathematicians, he appreciates an elegant solution to a challenging problem—logic and proofs are necessary. It was somewhat surprising that he decided to seek advice from someone who wouldn't be considered "logical" or "science-based." We spoke by phone in the summer of 2002.

"I'm calling about our children. We want what's best for them. We read about you. My wife and I were very impressed with what was written about you in that article. We were hoping to get your advice."

"I'm happy to help you. I hope you have stamina and patience."

"What do you mean?"

"In order to help you, we'll have to solve a few other problems first."

"That's fine. But I don't have any problems. I'm calling about our children and their education."

"I understand. Once again I need your assurance that you'll be patient and that you won't give up."

Michael is an orderly man, but he wasn't prepared for what was coming in his life. I needed to prepare him. During our second phone conversation, I addressed an issue that I knew he would have to deal with immediately.

"How's your wife?"

"You asked me this last time. She's fine. Why?"

"Actually, your wife needs professional attention."

I gave him a moment to think about this and then I had to address a larger problem.

"You seem to have your life very well planned out, but you didn't make room for illnesses or interruptions."

He was taken aback. I needed him to step back. I needed him to be less controlling and more compassionate. There was a much bigger issue in his life that needed my help. I felt his resistance. Nonetheless, he decided to cooperate and made his first break from his carefully thought out agenda.

"Actually, my wife is right here. Would you like to speak with her?"

"Yes. There's something I need to tell her."

His wife got on the phone. She was nervous, but I could sense that she had more belief, or faith, in my ability than he did.

"Do you see anything about our children? My daughter, my son?" she asked.

"I know how important they are to you and I'll do everything I can to help them succeed. Your children have two, wonderful, concerned parents. They have everything they need to make a good start in life. There's a bit of difference between them, but you probably don't want me to mention that right now."

This was a very sensitive matter in their family. I could see that their son had serious developmental challenges and that they didn't know how to deal with it. They'd been given a medical diagnosis for him that seemed irrefutable. I was ready to refute. A mistake had been made, which led to a simplistic diagnosis. I needed to help correct this, but it wasn't the right time. First, I needed their trust. I needed to get their lives in order so that they could deal with their most painful challenge.

"You want me to say that in the end everything will be fine. But before I do that, for your children to be fine, I need *you* to be fine."

I paused for her to absorb what I was saying. And then I had to move on.

"There's something physically wrong inside you."

Naturally, she was very disturbed by what I said.

"How can you sense there's something wrong with me when you haven't even met me?" she said, trying to hold her composure. "This is the first time we're speaking!"

"I can understand your doubt. You must understand that you play a large role in your children's life. We are discussing their success; therefore, you are part of that sphere. That's why I need you to go to the doctor for an examination. There's something that needs to be taken care of."

"What are you trying to say?" She began to stammer. "What is it?"

"The wonderful thing about this information is that, at this point, I see things *before* they occur, the first stages. If you have faith and a little trust, you'll do as I ask and have a check-up."

The wife was very shaken by this information. She politely said goodbye and put her husband back on the phone. I could feel his irritation.

"Is this something you had to do?"

"Yes."

"I don't know if it's true but ..." his voice trailed off. I could feel his skepticism.

"It sounds very amazing to me. We'll go, and I hope we'll give you a good report."

"Either way," I said, "in the end it will be fine."

There was a bit of patronizing laughter in his voice when he asked, "Do you think maybe we should see each other person-to-person?"

"That isn't important now."

We said goodbye and hung up.

I went to my favorite chair in the living room; I feel protected there. I asked myself, "Where am I headed with this? This wasn't the reason why they called. Why go through this?" The answer was simple: This is their time to come into my life. It's my responsibility to take care of those who come to me. I can prevent things, avoid them, see and advise, listen and guide. The love and concern I feel for people—that's what matters in life.

They called a few days later. He spoke first. He was quite agitated.

"Something *is* wrong. I can't believe this. If it wasn't for you ..."

The doctors discovered the life-threatening health matter that I knew needed immediate attention.

"There are many reasons why you called. There's much more in your life that I need to deal with."

Although I managed to impress him with my ability, I knew he was going to be a challenge because of his way of thinking.

"You have an agenda for everything, a life all laid out. I must advise that life isn't that way. No matter how well we plan our life, things change. There would've been a very big change in your life and the lives of your children if you hadn't taken the time to look after your wife."

Then, the wife spoke. I could hear a bit more fear in her voice.

"The news isn't all good."

I had to disagree.

"Yes, it is. It's just a matter of a few months. A few things need to be done. Everything will be fine. However, *you must not take your life for granted.* Without you, the success of your children can't be complete."

Fortunately, her husband was beginning to accept what I had to say.

"If you say it will be all right, I guess it will."

Sadly, he didn't want me to know how appreciative he was, which is something I encounter often.

"I'll call you in a few weeks," the wife promised.

"Take care of yourself," Michael said with true concern for me.

A few weeks later he called again.

"Things are going so well," he said. His wife was much better.

And this is something that always amazes me. Despite obvious proof of my ability with my diagnosis of her condition, she still didn't want to put all her trust in me. But she had faith nonetheless.

Michael returned to the topic of the children.

"About our daughter ..."

"We'll deal with your daughter later. But now you must not pressure her."

He wanted to talk more, but realized it was better to end the conversation. He didn't *want* to know more. Understandable. He was celebrating the success of his wife's escape from tragedy.

He called again about a month later.

"How are you? I've tried calling. You've been so busy! I understand. One question: My son ..."

I cut him off.

"No, we must set him aside for now."

Thankfully, Michael decided not to argue with me.

"Is there something else you need to say?"

I had to prepare him for another unexpected development that was coming.

"Yes. When are you moving? Have you decided what your next job is?"

His shock was considerable, and he immediately shared his discomfort and confusion.

"Moving? I have no intention of moving. My job? It's not the best, but I'm older and ..."

"Old?" I snapped.

Michael responded politely but firmly. "I'm in my job and that's where I'll stay. I had different goals in the past, but it just didn't work out. I'll stick to what I have."

"You must look at the reality and be willing to take action. No matter how much you try, you're not appreciated where you are. No matter what you say or do, you're not happy there. Don't allow people to stop your motivation. Be prepared to let them go."

"First of all: I have my son, my daughter, my wife, and my work. I can't change my situation. They're my responsibility. Second: Why would I want to let go of something that's steady? There's nothing at work that's upsetting me!"

"Be prepared because things could change."

Again, he was irritated.

"Well, if things change, I'll be sure to inform you."

"Thank you. I'm sure you will."

"I called you for something else—my son. What can we hope for him?"

I would not budge. It was important to stay on this frustrating track focusing on Michael.

"Why don't you allow life to take its course? Stop working with that agenda of yours."

At this point the wife got into the conversation.

"Should I prepare for anything? Is my boy going to be all right? Is my daughter going to school? Will she decide what she's going to do?"

Since I didn't feel any immediate urgency with the children, I concentrated on what I knew was going to be a tremendous challenge.

"Don't worry. Let's deal with things you never thought you'd be facing at this time." And then I decided to go for it. "If I were you, I'd start to pack."

She resisted.

"It's not that I don't believe in you, but we're so set in our ways. We're settled."

"I appreciate your honesty. Try to put your trust in me. You'll see."

It wasn't too long before the husband called again in a very agitated state.

"I'm going through a very difficult time," he said.

"Say no more. Why are you wasting your time on people who have broken your dreams, on people who can't see who you are or where you're headed? You're still the creative man you've always been. They've never really given you the opportunity to show who you are."

I paused just long enough for that statement to sink in.

"You've lost your job, yes?"

"Yes!"

He was desperate. He stuttered. He was lost, hurt, like a child who's afraid of his first day at school. Then I created an alternative agenda.

"Let's concentrate on your goals, on your life, on an everyday task. Let's set *your* agenda aside and let's start a new one. You can start by packing your things! We need to start with the idea that there's a trip involved."

I had to inspire him with my excitement and enthusiasm. I spoke as though we were a team.

"We need to walk into a new room. There will be interviews. We must present ourselves like we know who we are. We need to *show* the ability that we've been hiding inside. Other people *didn't* want to hear it or see it. We must allow new people to see the new *you*. We must show confidence and trust in ourselves. Work with me!"

He was silent.

"I give it three months. We'll help you remember who you are."

And with absolute certainty, I told him, "Trust me. Everything will be fine."

The wife was completely bewildered, even hurt.

"Why did this happen to us now?"

"Don't ask why. It's time to deal with this. Let him look inside himself. Michael! Can you hear what I'm trying to say?"

He heard, but he couldn't understand.

"I'm trying very hard to hear what you're saying."

It was time to turn a negative into a positive.

"Why have you accepted this event this way? Why do you see this as failure? Why do you see it as unfair? Why do I see it so differently? I see it as an opportunity of a lifetime! This is what you needed to happen in order to find yourself. And to see, even if they did not, that who you *are*, who they tried *to change*, who you *wanted to be* and they didn't allow, is a man with dreams and vision! They wouldn't permit that! Your suggestions were moved aside and someone else took advantage of them and got the credit."

I paused for a moment.

"But you were afraid of speaking up. Afraid of what? Afraid of losing what?"

"My job, of course!"

"A job?" I asked. "A job has to be like everything important in our lives, a place where we feel satisfied, trusted, and appreciated, a place where our words are heard!"

He still didn't understand.

"We need to find ourselves in a marriage, in a place where we fit, where we can be who we are, a place that will allow us to grow and make mistakes, allow us to correct those mistakes and move ahead."

He was too stunned to respond.

"Why don't you see it as I see it?" I shouted. "Why don't you see it as your first day of *freedom*?"

The logic was unassailable, but logic means nothing to a person who feels beaten and hopeless.

"You'll be able to be the man that I know you are. You'll prepare yourself. You'll introduce yourself to the people who will come into your life. You'll introduce them to your abilities, yourself, your courage, your faith, your motivation."

Finally, he answered with a question.

"That's what you see?"

"It will take three months. There will be four interviews. You'll probably only do three. You'll be invited back twice for all three interviews and that will be it. It won't be today, or tomorrow. It will take three months. Everything will be fine."

"How do you know?" he asked.

The wife, who had been listening patiently on the other line, stopped him.

"Why are you questioning? Don't you remember what she's done for us?"

"It's not questioning, it's fear."

"Have no fear. Sometimes we fear the things we can't see, and we accept the things we *do* see even though we know they're wrong. Even though we know we shouldn't be in a place, or with someone, or doing what we're doing. That's because it's become a part of our life. Because we feel accepted. Because we've grown used to it."

He responded with skepticism and bitterness.

"Do you think I can get a promotion at my age?"

"Yes, you will! You'll make more money than you're making now. Before you get to that, you must *look at yourself*! You must believe in yourself. You must respect your abilities, the things that you know to be true. You must not allow others to erase those thoughts or those ideas. Do you understand? The man who I see is a man who trusts himself, who doesn't need to hear it from others because he knows what he can do and accomplish."

He started to turn the corner.

"Yes, I know that man. I used to be that man."

"What happened?"

"He had a bad time at work."

I paused for him to consider that statement. Then I asked, "Do you have to stay in that job, no matter what you have to go through, because someone pays you?"

"Well it's the money. Not just money, it's the bills, the family. I'm a very responsible man!"

He was paralyzed by the shame of not honoring his responsibilities.

"Don't confuse responsibility with faith and trust in yourself. You don't understand what has happened in the past. I do. I don't want to give any energy to the past, the negativity. They overlooked you so many times."

I knew he needed an explanation.

"You needed to go through all of that so you could arrive where you are today."

I repeated my agenda.

"So, there will be three companies and they're in the following cities." I named them. "And you'll have to transfer. It's a familiar place. You've lived there before."

I repeated with emphasis:

"You must look at yourself. You must have faith in yourself."

And then I asked what any hiring executive would ask: "How can *I* have faith in you if *you* don't have faith in yourself?"

And then I gave him his assignment.

"You need to trust in yourself. You must set goals for what you want, set them, and realize them! No one else will give that to you. Only you can give that to yourself."

A couple of weeks later, he called with great excitement.

"It happened just like you said. I was invited back for a second meeting."

This is the most satisfying part of the work I do. He found faith in himself. *He practiced every day to have faith in himself.* He understood that all the years of preparation and hard work were finally paying off. A few days later, he called.

"The offer is amazing! Wonderful! They want me."

We were all happy and excited.

"When setting goals, you must give them the chance to develop and set aside time so you can achieve them. You must practice knowing yourself every day and believing in yourself! Then you can help those around you. It pays off. If you know who you are, it doesn't matter what others think. If you don't belong in certain surroundings, no matter how long you try to stay, the time will come when you'll have to leave."

"Thank you so much. You've made a new man of me."

"Your trust, faith, and dedication have made you the man you are *supposed* to be. The potential was always in you."

"Is there anything else you need to tell me?"

This was the moment I'd been waiting for.

"My purpose in your life is not what we've already done. I'm in your life for your son."

"My son?" he asked, slightly bewildered.

"Yes. This is a very important time in his life."

I tied it all together.

"Now he has a better chance. You're his father. You've changed your fixed ideas about life as you think it *should be*. You must see life as *it is*. *You must live in the moment*. You also needed to see your life from a position of strength. You'll understand your son and his special needs much better now that you've changed as a man. We can now deal with his needs because you've personally experienced the power of maintaining hope and faith in a seemingly hopeless situation."

I knew that his son would very soon be one of my biggest challenges.

Being a good person doesn't guarantee that good things will come to you as a reward for your goodness. The world we live in is complex. Be prepared to experience both good and bad in your life as you would day and night.

JIMMY

Thirty-four-year-old Jimmy was about to face a challenge that would have far reaching consequences in his life. He would need more than guidance from me because his natural optimism about life and people, coupled with his desire for independence, would lead him to make choices that were naïve at best. He was so sure of his pure intentions that he would often do things that were good for others but not necessarily good for him.

Jimmy was blessed with generosity of spirit. He felt so fortunate that he never doubted that life would be glorious. Jimmy also had an unusual advantage in life, one that raised many questions for him as a young boy growing up. "Why can my mother see things before they happen? How is that possible? What do I do with that information?"

Jimmy was our first baby. My husband and I adored him. He was a lovable, sweet child. I would cry with joy just looking at his innocent face. As he grew, so did the bond between us. He helped with everything, including taking care of his younger siblings, Billy and Peter. Peter, our youngest, needed a lot of extra care because he was born with some physical challenges.

Jimmy was there to help at every stage of Peter's development. He would build Peter's confidence by showing pride in his little brother. They would walk together wherever they went. Jimmy's optimistic attitude gave Peter the strength he would need in dealing with a harsh, judgmental world. Jimmy counteracted that negativity by giving Peter unconditional love. And, of course, Peter adored Jimmy for it.

Jimmy was also a great friend to those around him. He liked people and thought the best of them. It was hard to convince him that there were people in the world who did not have his best interests in mind. And, like most young people, he was oblivious to danger. I was often torn between warning him of impending danger and letting him learn certain lessons on his own no matter how much I wanted to protect him. I remember one incident when he was in his late teens.

"Jimmy! I don't think you should ride in that car today. In fact, you should tell your friend to leave his car at home."

Jimmy did not heed that warning, even though he knew that my warnings were not to be ignored. He needed to discover two things for himself: Is my mother infallible? Am I my own man or am I a mama's boy?

I was very anxious that afternoon. I knew something bad was going to happen. As expected, the phone rang. It was the police.

"Your son has been in a serious car accident. He was taken to the hospital."

I immediately sensed that there was something inaccurate about what the officer was thinking; there was another side to the story. I thanked him, hung up the phone and asked Bill to drive me to the hospital. When we arrived at the Emergency Room, Bill happened to notice Jimmy's jacket at the nurse's station. It was soaked with blood. Bill began to panic, but I told him to remain calm.

"It's not what you think." To the nurses, I said, "That's not my son's blood," which completely confused the nurses. Before they could say anything, I headed straight down the hall toward one of the rooms. They tried to stop me.

"Where are you going? Your son is in Intensive Care. Come back."

I knew where he was, and it wasn't Intensive Care. I could feel him. I rushed down the hall and chose the room that I knew he was in. I entered and found Jimmy sitting up in bed. He had a few scratches on his blushing face. I felt his shame for not listening to me. Unfortunately, it was his friend who paid the heaviest price. He was the one in Intensive Care. It was his blood that covered Jimmy's jacket. Fortunately, his friend survived. Things worked out well—that time. I knew that they wouldn't always work out well.

After graduating from high school, Jimmy attended college and then continued his education by enlisting in the United States Navy during the Persian Gulf War.

Jimmy loved his country. I'm opposed to any form of war, but Jimmy believed that it was his duty to serve his country. It was non-negotiable.

He served with distinction and became a decorated veteran. Immediately after the war, he developed some health problems with his lungs, as did several of his mates. This illness was only the beginning of his physical troubles. On his first day of leave

back in San Francisco, overjoyed at being back in his home-
land, he had the uncontrollable urge to indulge a fantasy. He
bought a motorcycle. It happened to be my birthday. He called
with great excitement in his voice.

"Happy birthday, Ma! Can't wait to see you!"

I listened but knew that his future wasn't going to be as simple as that.

"Jimmy. Listen to me. Are you planning on taking any trips
today?"

"Heck no, Ma."

"Jimmy. It's very important that you don't do anything with
a motorcycle. Do you understand me?"

"Don't worry, Ma. I'm not going to do anything dangerous."

I nodded. It's funny when people develop a strong desire for
something. They can't conceive of something bad happening if
their desire is innocent and pure. I knew he wanted to impress
me with his fearless independence. I would have to suffer what
was coming.

After hanging up, despite Jimmy's assurances, I told Bill to
pack a bag because we were going to be taking a trip the next
day. Bill didn't understand what I was talking about.

"Jimmy's going to be here in a few days!"

Despite Bill's frustration with me and my predictions, he
knew me well enough to pack his bag as I had requested. I
didn't tell him that I knew something awful involving a motorcycle was going to take place. I saw the accident vividly in my
mind.

Jimmy ignored my warning. After all, how dangerous could a motorcycle be compared to war? My attempt to change that destiny failed.

The next day we were on a plane bound for San Diego where Jimmy was already fighting for his life in a military hospital. The nurses later told me that a car had run a red light and struck him on his new motorcycle. I looked at my baby lying helpless on the hospital bed, tubes in and out of all parts of his body. I could barely see his face. Blood was seeping through the bandages that were wrapped around his battered skull. The doctors had implanted a metallic shunt in his head to protect his exposed brain. They informed me that he was semi-comatose and unable to move his limbs. The prognosis was grim.

Despite the very best medical experts and equipment available to the military, any substantial recovery was out of the question. The doctors gave up hope. I refused to accept this verdict. I signed for his release and took on the challenge of my son's rehabilitation. I began by taking him away from the hopeless attitude of the doctors and brought him back to the powerful energy of his family. One should never underestimate the power of love, hope, and prayer. Jimmy was enveloped with the healing powers of his home and family. With careful nursing from all of us, a complex two-year rehabilitation proved successful.

I won't go into the details of what we had to do for Jimmy. The point is that I knew I could get him back. It wasn't Jimmy's time yet.

A slow-but-steady eight-year convalescence followed. Jimmy recovered despite the doubts of all the experts. But I also knew that Jimmy's trials were far from finished.

Jimmy was able to live a somewhat normal life. The one thing missing was a relationship, a woman. With his recovered health, the normal appetites of any young man also returned. Jimmy entered a casual relationship with a young woman who he was somewhat acquainted with in the neighborhood. What began as casual very quickly transformed into something quite intense and serious. I advised him to move slowly with this new friendship, not only because of the delicate state of his health, but because I could see that this relationship could change his life dramatically.

"We're just friends, Ma," he said.

But I saw something much different. She was from a family with many challenges. As I read her, I could see that life had presented her with very difficult obstacles, none of which were her creation. She had to grow up much faster than other young girls, and the consequences of that premature responsibility were evident in her behavior. It was clear that advice from me was unwelcome; not uncommon for girls her age. She wanted to show her independence and maturity. But when she met Jimmy and experienced the love and unity of our family, she reveled in what had been missing in her life. Once again, it wasn't as simple as just experiencing that, which she had been lacking at home. She needed to do a lot of work to heal. I didn't tell Jimmy all of this, but I did warn him to be careful. I decided long ago that I wanted my children to live their lives without the claustrophobic feeling of being constantly watched by me.

They needed to create their own lives. I would help only if they asked for it.

Jimmy was being led by a very powerful physical need. On their very first date, his passion and newly discovered vitality overwhelmed his reason. It wasn't long before she became pregnant. She gave birth to two children in rapid succession. His life was irrevocably changed.

Jimmy loved his wife very much. The gift of their wonderful children was all he wanted from life. No matter how many challenges, no matter how much they argued, he always felt that life was wonderful and that they could overcome any obstacle. Jimmy no longer lived for himself; he lived and worked for his family. Unfortunately, despite his commitment, his wife could not form a better future with him because her stormy past remained part of her present. Her true nature had never been nurtured. She was recreating her past without realizing it. What could have been an easy relationship instead continued as an ongoing battle for both of them. Peace and satisfaction would never be attained.

Regardless, Jimmy would not accept defeat. He tried everything in his power to create happiness for his family. He vowed that nothing would stand in the way of his goal. Unfortunately, all the determination in the world could not change what was coming. A painful vision came to me one night as we played Bingo.

Suffering is part of the journey of life. Don't live in fear of it. When you feel that life has been particularly cruel to you, think of others who have suffered as much if not more than you. You must fight to survive despite unimaginable pain. Wisdom is born from the labor of transcending difficult experiences.

ELIZABETH

People often wonder why I seem to have inappropriate emotional responses to events that occur. When some cry, I am silent. When others express joy, I cry. You see, by the time these events occur I've already shed my tears or laughed my laugh. I've experienced the event before it takes place. I say my goodbyes before it's time. I prepare for hellos before I meet the person I know I'll meet. It's a difficult ability to live with. It was never more difficult than this one time in my life. I was able to see an event in my son's future that caused me indescribable pain. But my duty to him, to his wife, their children, and to my family was to prepare them for what had to be.

It was October, approximately three years after the birth of Jimmy's second child. The leaves on the trees outside his home were transforming to the vibrant colors that emerge before they inexorably must fall to the ground for the next cycle of life. Our entire family was inside the house having a wonderful day. As the sun was setting outside, we were playing Bingo in their cozy kitchen. My husband was on my right, as he always is, and Peter was next to him. Billy was on my left. Jimmy was straight across from me and his wife was next to him. We loved playing games together as a family. But this day would be different. I was in charge of calling the numbers.

"B-10!"

I looked up at my son. He was so happy. And with that happiness I saw the sign. It was the sign that I was very familiar with but never dreaded. I saw the light from the side of my eye that always appears before the inevitable. It was unmistakable. It was his time. I felt ill, but I knew I had to speak. I called his attention.

"Jimmy!"

"Yeah, Mom?" He answered with his customary loving tone.

"Jimmy." I was fighting to contain my emotions. I had to be strong.

"It's time," I said gently. "Do you understand me?"

Everyone was silent.

Jimmy looked at me in disbelief. There was a long silence as the meaning of my words became clear to him and everyone at the table. It was a terrible moment. Jimmy's eyes were filled with hurt and confusion. I knew that he wanted to ask, "How could you let this happen to someone you love? We know your power—do something! Don't let this happen." But he just looked at me, waiting.

I will always honor Jimmy because no one had as much faith in me as my son. But faith and power have nothing to do with leaving this world if it's your time. I could only prepare him and the family for the acceptance of death.

Bill was furious.

"Mom! Stop it!" he growled.

"No, no. We must prepare ourselves," I said, closing my eyes, trying not to reveal my own feelings. I hated my gift at that moment. The only way I could contain my pain was by continuing. I had to press forward. I returned to the game.

"G-40."

There was a short silence. Jimmy's wife attempted to shift the mood of the room.

"What your mother is saying is that we have to take Jimmy to the doctor." She often interpreted my predictions. She didn't want to believe in my ability, nor did she want Jim to believe in it. She felt the need to compete with me for Jim's devotion. It was a natural attempt to exercise some control over Jim.

"We can stop this," she said, referring to the "illness." I understood what she was doing and why she was doing it. After all, why would they want to believe it?

Bill agreed.

"You've got to take care of yourself, Jim! Prevention, man!"

This optimistic talk seemed to calm everyone. That couldn't change what I knew was coming. So, we continued the game. They decided I was in one of my moods. It wasn't until everyone went to bed that my husband gently asked me if it was necessary to upset everyone with my prediction.

"Yes," I answered. "I have to say it as I see it. We mustn't fear death. We must make the best of the time we have left. We must prepare."

Five months later, I was flying home from San Francisco after one of my consultations. I called Jimmy from the airplane.

"Jimmy! I want to celebrate my birthday with you."

He was a bit confused by this.

"Mom, your birthday isn't until August."

"I want to celebrate my birthday with you," I repeated.

"Okay, Ma. You know that I love you."

I wanted to make Jimmy as happy as I could possibly make him. He indulged me.

That weekend he came home. I made his favorite dinner, a huge batch of ribs. We invited everybody to the house. We celebrated. Everybody laughed and ate. Everyone was happy. My prediction was forgotten.

It was a few days after that celebration that Jimmy's illness manifested in its true form. He suddenly had great difficulty breathing. We immediately made a doctor's appointment. His wife was concerned but kept insisting, "Jimmy is far too young and strong to be at risk of dying." I, however, knew with absolute certainty that it was the week before his death. I asked him to come home.

"I can't, Ma," he answered. "I have too many obligations." His wife had work. He was torn, but Jimmy never wanted to disappoint me, so he came the next day.

I told him, "You should stay here in your room. Stay with us. And your brothers should stay also." And they did. No matter how much they didn't want to believe me, they decided it would be better to be close to him just in case he was in need. The room rang with laughter as they watched baseball and joked. Everything seemed fine.

Jimmy's wife visited with the kids. She struggled to honor my request even though it caused disruption in her household routine. Peter, who never doubts me, made sure to spend every moment with Jimmy. It wasn't because he believed my prediction (he couldn't even begin to accept the possibility of Jimmy's death); it was out of love for his brother.

Billy decided that Jimmy was "looking so good" that he rescheduled his plans to go out with a friend.

"You should stay here," I said. But Billy had already decided that everything was fine. I looked at him carefully. "I really think you should stay."

He wasn't happy, but he honored my wish. My husband, however, went out to run an errand. He was in the same state of denial. No one could allow themselves to believe it would happen.

Jimmy's wife kept calling him to ask when he was coming home. She knew that there was no point in arguing with Jimmy when it came to me, so she tolerated the inconvenience. She was convinced that I was seeing a warning vision.

I just focused on my son's happiness.

At one point, Jimmy asked if we could change a doctor's appointment we had made earlier in the week.

"No," I said. "That we must do."

Jimmy was disappointed. I hated disappointing him, but it was necessary. He, too, could not comprehend what was coming. We were getting closer to the inevitable. I stayed with him in his room. I needed to stay with him once more. Every moment was so precious for me. We talked about many things from the past, about his difficult birth, what a good boy he was, what a good brother he was, the good times we had. We were saying goodbye without saying it. We didn't talk about his family, children, or wife, but he did ask if I would remember to tell them things about him when he was no longer here.

"Of course I will."

"Remember how many chicken wings I was able to eat?"

We laughed. And then we became very quiet. He was beginning to recognize the change in his body and what it could mean.

"And now I can't even eat one."

We sat in silence for a short while trying not to think of the reason why we were there. It was awkward for him and incredibly painful for me. Finally, Jimmy decided to watch TV. He asked if he could put his head on my lap like he used to do when he was little. I smiled even as I felt my heart breaking. We sat together and I stroked his hair the way I had done so many times when he was growing up. It was a bittersweet moment. I remember thinking to myself, "How lucky I am—to know in advance."

The next morning, my husband got up and went out to run more errands. Nothing seemed out of the ordinary. Bill had promised he would drive us to the doctor's appointment after his work. It was an ordinary day.

It wasn't more than an hour later when Jimmy called out to me. He was white as a sheet. He could barely breathe or move. I called Bill at work.

"You've got to come. Jimmy's much worse."

Bill drove his car up to the house beyond the driveway and right to the front door. He ran into the house, picked Jimmy up in his arms and took him to the car. On his way, Bill glared at me. He was thinking, "How could you let this happen?"

We raced to the hospital. When we got to the Emergency Room, the doctor told me that everything would be all right and that we should relax. Jimmy would be just fine; he was a young man and would certainly pull through. They needed to put something like a pacemaker in his chest. After the procedure, we went to see him. Jimmy was sitting up in bed, very chipper and talking about things he was going to do later in the week.

"Look, Ma! Now I know what you were so worried about. But see? I'm so much better!"

I could see. I understood that he was better—for the moment. I always found it remarkable that the body feels so much better just before the end. But there was no point in saying any of that.

My husband decided that the emergency had passed. He wanted to pick up Peter from school and bring him to the hospital. There was no point stopping him; he didn't need to witness what was coming.

I took the doctor by the arm, looked him in the eyes and said, "If there's any change whatsoever, I'll be sitting out here waiting.

"Please." I held his arm. "Please tell me if there's any change in his condition."

"It's nothing," he assured me, patting my hand. "Everything will be okay. I really don't think this is anything serious."

"I'm not a doctor or anything," I said. "But please. If there's the slightest change, please let me know immediately."

Bill and I sat in the Waiting Room. He was feeling very optimistic and relieved. He called Jimmy's wife at work to explain what had happened, that we were waiting at the hospital, and that Jimmy was recovering. There was nothing I could say at that moment that would have made what was coming any easier. Twenty minutes later, a nurse came walking toward us. She was holding Jimmy's neck chain with the Navy Cross that he had been awarded.

"He said to give it to his brother Bill."

The blood drained from Bill's face.

"He said that you should keep it."

She gave it to him with particular care. She could see by his reaction that this was more significant than she realized. She excused herself, sensing the awkwardness of the moment.

I could feel Bill's anguish. He stared at the chain as it rested in his hand. He was angry. He refused to accept the possibility of death.

"He listens to you too much, Ma," he said bitterly, as though I was the cause of these events. But Bill knew. He knew that *I don't cause events; I see them.* He knew that Jimmy would never have parted with that chain unless something was very wrong. He knew in his heart that I never take back what I say. He knew from too many past experiences that my words always proved to be true. He also knew that if I could have changed the course of events that I would have. He was beginning to believe what I said would be inevitable.

It must have been ten minutes later that the doctor came out with a very concerned and confused look on his face.

"I don't understand," he stammered. "There's something very wrong."

I bypassed the doctor and ran to Jimmy's room. He was in bed, barely conscious. It was time. I don't know how to describe the pain in my heart. My precious child was dying and there was nothing I could do. I was powerless. My gift was useless. No amount of begging, crying or praying was going to change what was occurring. I felt paralyzed with pain as I watched his body shutting down. He was going quickly. And so, I thanked God for preparing me. I thanked Him for allowing me to sob privately. I had experienced my heartbreak before. It was time for me to help Jimmy. All I could do was help him go with peace of mind.

I gently cradled Jimmy in my arms and said loudly so that he could hear me.

"Jimmy! Jimmy! Look at me! Look at Mommy!" He opened his eyes. "Jimmy! It's all right. Don't worry. Everything will be all right. Do you understand?"

"But, Ma," he whispered, struggling for breath.

I assured him. "The children, everything! You don't have to worry. Give Mommy a kiss and you can go now."

He looked me in the eyes. He could barely focus, but he managed to see me. We said goodbye with our eyes, we kissed, and I felt his spirit leave his body. My beloved child was gone.

As I held my baby's lifeless body, I prayed for him. The tears streamed again.

Our family was devastated. It was finally time for them to cry. My husband, Peter, and Bill stood by the bed and wept bitterly.

When Bill was finally able to control his tears, he called Jimmy's wife. She became angry. She accused Bill of making a joke of something very serious. His pain-filled voice assured her that it was true. It was time for her to believe also.

Premature death of a child is hard to accept. For a mother it's unthinkable. But one must accept that those decisions are not in our hands. Therefore, rather than feel sorry for ourselves, rather than rage at our misfortune, rather than stop living, we must find the strength to accept the pain and understand how to truly honor the spirit who leaves us on this plane of existence. Mine were the first eyes he saw when he was born, and they were the last when his life ended. I'm grateful for that final moment. I learned something else that day: The life journey is not only finished when life comes to an end, it's also finished when we lose hope. We must never lose hope.

REALITY

I didn't say any of this would be easy. Are you looking for a life without struggle? Stop looking! We all suffer. It's *part* of life. Take comfort in the fact that you are one of billions who struggle against challenges that are painful. I see them every day. There is *no one* who does not suffer in his or her lifetime. Since you can't bypass it, you might as well be strong for when it comes. I have seen greatness in those who have learned to accept suffering. It's *how* you deal with pain that makes all the difference. If all you do is feel sorry for yourself, you'll never learn the most important lesson: *Life is filled with challenges that you must learn to overcome.*

MY WISH

I look at you. I look into your eyes. I see beyond the veil of confusion where your hope and pure spirit wait for liberation. I see your soul, your desire. I see where and when your life stood still. I see you before you were afraid to take a chance. I remind you of what once meant a lot to you. It could have been a moment, a thought, a feeling; both positive and negative. We start working with those elements and then we bring out the person who is hidden beneath them. We bring out the *pure potential* that's already there.

THE POWER OF YOUR MIND

The human mind is truly miraculous. Look around you! Can you imagine life without the extraordinary inventions of humankind? Who could have imagined the technology that we live with today? Dreamers! What makes a computer work? What's the magic behind cell phones and self-driving cars? Visionaries! How is it that we're able to send extensions of ourselves to different planets? Our virtual hands and eyes have been on Mars, Jupiter, and beyond! How is it possible that we can see or speak to a person halfway around the world? Achievers! How is it possible that my mind can see deep into your past and far into your future? How do these things happen? This is the power of the human mind—inexplicable manifestations of ideas and visions, but very clearly there. We're able to travel in space and return to share what we've discovered. We can cure illness and prolong life. We can see the unseen. We can change what we wish to change. The mind has extraordinary potential that we've only begun to tap.

Imagine the power of your mind if it chooses to construct a negative belief. *It will be realized by the force of your mind.* Do you see? Do you understand the power you possess? You are in charge of how things can be. I want you to harness this power to get you off the path of negativity and on the path of happiness and success. This power is yours! Don't permit yourself to do anything less than realize your full potential.

Ninety-nine percent of the people I meet suffer from a lack of confidence. You can overcome this if you're willing to *help yourself.* Use the infinite power of your mind and put yourself on a positive course.

Now you've been given a second chance, let's forget the chance that didn't work so well. But if you give up when you're given a second chance then the fault is yours.

My mission is for people to understand that when you make the decision to change, everything will change with you. Enjoy the adventure of your exploration. Begin your magnificent quest.

"We can't solve problems by using the same kind of thinking we used when we created them."

—ALBERT EINSTEIN

IN CLOSING

You may need my help. We may not have met yet. Don't let that stop you. Remember that there's a great deal of work you can do on your own. Begin the work because life rewards those who are willing to work hard at changing life patterns that aren't working. You must do the work. Begin with the guidance I've given you in this book.

If our paths are to cross, please understand my purpose. I will understand and accept what you're hiding or what you long for without a word exchanged or any question asked. Your pain will reflect in my face and your joy in my heart.

"Will this last?" you will ask. And, as quickly, I will answer.

There is more to light than some can see. The worst fear in life is to fear oneself, one's actions, one's decisions, and one's thoughts. Therefore, I must become you in order to understand what it is that you do not say, that thing that holds you back from feeling happiness and holds you back from feeling complete.

The world is not the way we want it to be, but we must find it in ourselves the purpose of our existence and how we are to serve. There must be more to this life than just you.

I have found my purpose—to find the real you. I've done this so many times, and I will do it again many times more. I will take away your pain, give you a reason to live, and give you a reason to smile. I will show you your innocence. You knew these things but didn't want to accept them because of your fear. Why hear the negative so clearly, when the truth is right in front of you waiting to be unleashed?

CHALLENGES OF THE TWENTY-FIRST CENTURY

Your Hidden Truth deals primarily with your past and present. I want to look at your future.

The world is changing faster than ever, and it's also becoming more complex. It's a time of unrelenting advances in new technology, and a culture that leans toward antipathy rather than empathy. These are challenges we must face together.

Think how quickly your world has changed in the last twenty years. Did you ever imagine you'd be carrying an iPhone in your pocket? Did you ever think you'd be able to communicate with people in other parts of the world at the touch of a button? Did you ever imagine a world dominated by social media and the twenty-four-hour news cycle? Information is power, and information is exactly what we need—*useful information.*

My next book deals with some of the effects of the information age, and other advancements that continue to shape and serve the needs of society today. Children, parents, business people, artists, politicians—everyone is dealing with a world in which information spreads quickly. The possibilities for this type of technology are only limited by one's imagination. We need to prepare for unexpected developments in this ever-changing, insatiably curious and creative world, and we need to understand how its impact on different generations of people, some more technologically savvy than others by virtue of the way they grew up, has shaped our collective thinking.

Anyone over the age of thirty-five knows just how fast our world has changed. But for young people, it's all they've ever known. It's created a schism, and it's just the beginning. Technology, as well as our capacity to learn from it, is leaping forward at an unprecedented rate, but with many hidden pitfalls. We've seen it already. But this doesn't mean people are destined to fall into them. We're able to make choices about what we include and exclude from life. We need to prepare for what's already here and for what's coming. You don't need to have my ability to see that the world is a complicated place. But lots of people ignore it because they feel there's nothing they can change.

It's important to understand that this precarious world is not the creation of any single person, political party, country, or religion. It's the creation of many, many contributors over many, many years. It's a complex world, and there are no simple solutions. It's not about any one leader, one policy, or one institution. No one group is better than the other. No one person knows better than everyone else. We're in this together. We're related. We must treat each other with respect, without prejudice. We must acknowledge our connection to each other. It's reasonable. It's possible. And it's possible now, not later. It will take work, but harmony can happen one day.

Until that day comes, the world will continue to be a complicated place, full of disagreement and disappointment. It's up to us to make the best of the world by being aware of the beautiful gifts that come with it. When you're clear about who you are and where you came from, we'll continue the journey. We'll discover your destiny in the twenty-first century together.

ACKNOWLEDGEMENTS

This book would not be possible without the support of many dear friends. I wish to thank George de la Peña for the many hours of hard work we shared crafting it together, and my dear friend Doctor Ernesto Jonas, who believed in my ability even when he could not explain it. Though he has passed he will never be forgotten. I would like to thank all the wonderful people who offered their stories to help illustrate the power of this work. I want to thank George for inviting me to serve a purpose in the life of his friends, Patrick Swayze and Lisa Niemi. It was a privilege to help them through a challenging ordeal and to make a difference in their lives. In his inspiring book, *The Time of My Life*, he expressed thanks for my guidance. Thank you, Lisa and Patrick, for acknowledging me. I was particularly proud of Patrick for doing exactly what I espouse in this book—he fought for his dreams. And, throughout our brief relationship, he fought to prove me wrong. "I will beat this cancer. You'll see," he told me. And I understood. Beautiful Patrick—always fighting, never accepting defeat, and expressing love all at once.

I thank my husband and my sons, William and Peter, who mean everything to me. I also want to thank my grandchildren—James, Aaron, Christian, and Nicholas—for sacrificing precious time with their grandmother so she could help others.

ELIZABETH FOTINOPOULOS

With over 20 years of experience in the private and professional consultation business, Elizabeth Fotinopoulos has successfully transformed the lives and fortunes of many people in the United States and abroad. She is celebrated as one of the most gifted people in her field of psychic analysis. Her ability to identify and help overcome unseen obstacles in a person's life has been proven time and again.

"I always remind people that every problem has a solution if we are willing to acknowledge it."

Elizabeth is the proud mother of three sons and four grandchildren. Based in Long Island, New York, Elizabeth has shaped lives with insights that empower the client with a personal choice structure.

By providing people with a series of outcomes for each possible choice, Elizabeth believes people are granted a higher degree of awareness, setting the tone for dynamic lifetime effects. Her method engages each client with a unique level of interaction; never requiring tarot cards, personal items or common tools that stereotype most people who claim to be spiritual consultants.

"There is no limit to the type of individual I am prepared to help. They can be young or old, female or male, married or unmarried. The only condition to seeking advice from me is for you to truly want to change your life for the better."

Elizabeth has done community service by giving free sessions to gatherings of 500 to as many as 5,000 people.

"I value group gatherings because they allow me to enjoy a multitude of personalities where no two situations are alike."

Born and raised in New York City, Elizabeth has taken pride in many years of formal education. She was named valedictorian of her high school class and completed college soon after. Elizabeth also spent a long time working alongside her father, an attorney. Following her time working with her father, Elizabeth then went on her own and started working for General Motors, working her way up to the position of first female Service Director for General Motors in the United States and Europe. However, her true calling had been discovered at a young age.

Elizabeth discovered her connection with the part of life not visible to most at the age of five. Elizabeth was guided by the gentle hand of her grandmother who had similar abilities and by the support of her understanding family.

"My grandmother told me to never be afraid of the special and unusual things that God allowed me to see and feel," says Elizabeth. "The day when I realized I should use my ability to help others was an important one," Elizabeth said. "I truly enjoy making a difference in people's lives and cannot imagine a day without serving someone."

Elizabeth has served foreign and local dignitaries, celebrities, and high-level executives for some of the most respected Asian companies in the world. Even though Elizabeth is currently learning the Chinese language and works through the services of translators, she is fluent in Spanish, Greek, and English.